Agricultural Cooperatives in the U.S. and Israel

Comparative Performance of Cooperatives and Investor-Owned Firms

Zvi Lerman

Claudia Parliament

Dedication

This volume is dedicated to Yoav Kislev of the Hebrew University of Jerusalem, a great agricultural economist and a great friend, whose inspiration guided us in our research on cooperatives.

Table of Contents

Preface

This book is an outgrowth of four years of collaboration (1988-1992) between the two authors within the framework of a research project supported by BARD – U.S.-Israel Binational Agricultural Research and Development Fund. The idea of comparing the performance of cooperatives and investor-owned firms (IOFs) was suggested by the dramatic financial crisis that hit the cooperative agriculture in Israel in 1986 and almost bankrupted the entire agriculture sector. Was the crisis endemic to the Israeli economic system or was it engendered by the cooperative organizational and behavioral features of Israeli agriculture?

We tried to answer this question by running comparisons in two dimensions: comparing the performance of different organizational forms – cooperatives and IOFs in one country; and comparing the performance of the different organizational forms in two radically different economic environments – the U.S. and Israel.

Although the research was launched almost three decades ago, it was based on long time series of consistently comparable financial statements and we believe in the robustness of the results. The main conclusion of interest is that large, commercially oriented agricultural cooperatives perform not worse than IOFs in comparable circumstances and that the effect of cooperative specific-factors on performance, to the extent that it exists, is largely a function of the economic-cultural environment. We furthermore believe that the methodology used in our comparative analysis has withstood the test of time and the new generation of graduate students and researchers may benefit from getting acquainted with our approach. With this in mind, we have decided to put together the results of our research and offer them to the scholarly community in a single volume.

The people who encouraged us in the course of this research are too numerous to list. One name must be mentioned, however: our friend Yoav Kislev, a great agricultural economist from the Hebrew University of Jerusalem. Back in 1986, when we both were junior researchers, it was Yoav who got us interested in studying the performance of agricultural cooperatives and continued to follow our work with guidance and advice. Yoav also offered major inputs, both conceptual and factual, to Chapter 1 on the financial crisis in Israel's cooperative agriculture. This volume is dedicated to Yoav Kislev with gratitude and devotion.

Summary and Conclusions

Persistent overborrowing in Israeli cooperative agriculture led to a severe financial crisis in 1986. This overborrowing may have been caused by the moral-hazard behavior and horizon problems inherent to cooperative organizations. The hypothesis that cooperative-specific factors were responsible for the crisis is tested by examining the behavior of agricultural cooperatives in a culturally different environment (the U.S.) and by comparing the performance of cooperatives to that of investor-owned firms (IOFs).

From comparability considerations, cooperative performance is evaluated using standard financial ratios based on audited financial statements, which restricts the view of the cooperatives to a variant of a classical firm.

Contrary to theoretical expectations, agricultural cooperatives in the U.S. were found to perform as well as or better than comparable IOFs by profitability, leverage, and interest coverage measures. The proportion of new debt raised by cooperatives to finance new investment was not higher than in IOFs. No clear evidence was found of the hypothesized overinvestment in fixed assets or pronounced moral hazard behavior in U.S. cooperatives. The fact that U.S. cooperatives finance nearly half of their annual investment with equity funds does not support the hypothesis of "equity starvation" induced by horizon problems. The lack of significant differences in profitability between the two types of firms suggests that U.S. regional cooperatives may be following goals similar to IOFs.

Israeli agricultural cooperatives appear to have consistently followed a much riskier financial strategy than comparable U.S. cooperatives. Israeli cooperatives also use more debt than IOFs. The differences in strategic behavior of cooperatives in different countries, as reflected in capital structure and borrowing decisions, can be attributable to cultural-environmental factors, which are unquestionably reinforced by behavioral factors inherent to cooperative organizations. This suggests that even if the financial crisis in Israel was indeed precipitated by cooperative-specific factors, these factors are not universally active: their prominence or importance is largely a function of the cultural and economic environment.

1

Motivation and Objectives

The motivation for this joint U.S.–Israel research was provided by the traumatic experience that hit Israel's agriculture sector in 1986. Israeli agriculture is an agriculture of cooperatives: agricultural cooperatives cultivate 70 percent of all agricultural land and account for more than 80 percent of agricultural output in Israel.

Israeli agriculture is also a technological success story. During the last three decades (1960-1987), the agricultural product increased by a factor of 2.7 in constant domestic prices, net capital assets employed in agriculture increased by a factor of 1.7, and agricultural exports increased by a factor of 9.7 in US dollars. Total cultivated acreage in the same period remained static (although arable acreage increased) and agricultural labor declined more than 10 percent below the 1960 level. Yet, despite its impressive technological record, Israeli agriculture collapsed financially in 1985-86 in the sense that farmers simply could not continue servicing their debt.

It has been conjectured that, given the all-embracing cooperative structure of Israeli agriculture, its financial failure may have been attributable to cooperative-specific factors. An alternative point of view may be that the financial crisis was induced by general factors inherent to the economic environment in Israel and cooperative structure as such cannot be blamed. The present research tries to resolve this issue by a two-fold methodology: (a) by looking at the behavior of cooperatives in a different economic and cultural environment (the U.S.) and (b) by comparing the performance of agricultural cooperatives to that of non-cooperative investor-owned firms in related industries.

The report starts with an analysis of the 1986 financial crisis in Israeli cooperative agriculture that motivated this research. Then elements of the theory of cooperative behavior that provide the basis for the empirical work are surveyed. After a brief description of the database and the empirical methodology follow chapters that report the results on size and industry effects among U.S. agricultural cooperatives, comparative performance of agricultural cooperatives and investor-owned firms in the U.S. food industries, and financing of growth in U.S. agricultural cooperatives. The performance of Israeli regional cooperatives is similarly analyzed and compared to the performance of investor-owned firms in Israel. A comparison of the findings in U.S. and Israel follows; some conceptual conclusions are summarized in the last chapter.

1. Financial Crisis in Cooperative Agriculture in Israel[1]

1.1. Cooperative Organization of Israeli Agriculture

Modern Jewish agriculture developed as cooperative agriculture initially because of socialist ideology and later as a matter of public policy. The socialist ideology of cooperation was imported in the first decades of the 20th century by Zionist immigrants from Eastern Europe and Russia. They set the tone for the future by adopting the kibbutz (collective village) and the moshav (a comprehensive village-level cooperative association) as the preferred models of agricultural settlement.

The public policy of cooperation was adopted by the Zionist settling bodies in the pre-independence period (under the British Mandate in Palestine) because of the need to settle penniless immigrants without any farming experience on nationally owned land. This policy of cooperation was continued by the State of Israel after its establishment in 1948: development of agricultural settlements was considered a national priority of the new state and the waves of new immigrants had to be provided with all means of production, including startup capital and allotments of nationally owned land. Thus, although formally agricultural cooperation has always been voluntary, settlers had to organize in cooperatives in order to produce, unless they had independent resources. Public encouragement of cooperation was in fact responsible for the predominance of cooperatives in Israeli agriculture.

---

[1] This chapter has greatly benefited from inputs and advice from Yoav Kislev. For an updated overview, see Rosenthal and Eiges (2014).

Table 1.1 presents a schematic typology of agricultural cooperatives in Israel. The primary level – kibbutzim, collective moshavim (*moshav shitufi* in Hebrew), and moshavim – are multipurpose cooperatives engaged in a variety of activities, which also include agricultural production. They differ in the degree of cooperative control of consumption and production, while input purchasing and produce marketing are centrally organized in all primary cooperatives (at least in principle). The secondary level are the regional service cooperatives, the so-called "regional enterprises" – produce sorting, packing, and storage facilities, feed mills, grain elevators, cotton gins, poultry processing plants. Another type of secondary cooperative is the "purchasing organization" (*irgun kniyot* in Hebrew; "irgunim" in plural). Originally established to handle centralized input purchasing and produce marketing for their member cooperatives in each region, the purchasing organizations developed into powerful financial intermediaries raising bank credit and allocating it to their members.

TABLE 1.1: Types of Agricultural Cooperatives in Israel

A. PRIMARY COOPERATIVES

	Degree of cooperation			
	Consumption	Production	Purchasing/ marketing	Finance
Kibbutz	Yes	Yes	Yes	Yes
Collective moshav	No	Yes	Yes	Yes
Moshav	No	No*	Yes	Yes

B. SECONDARY COOPERATIVES

	Functions	Ownership structure
Regional enterprises	Primary agricultural services Secondary processing	Primary cooperatives Regional purchase organizations
Purchasing organizations	Purchasing/marketing Credit intermediation	Primary cooperatives Regional enterprises

* Scale crops (citrus orchards, wheat, cotton) are sometimes handled cooperatively also in the moshav.

The membership of the secondary cooperatives are the primary cooperatives in the corresponding region. Kibbutzim and moshavim as a rule maintain separate secondary cooperative organizations in each region, and the collective moshavim usually join the kibbutz regional cooperatives because of greater organizational affinity. The ownership structure of regional service cooperatives ("regional enterprises") does not follow a uniform pattern: some regional enterprises are owned directly by the primary member cooperatives (on patronage principles), while others are owned by the regional purchasing organization, which in turn is owned by the primary cooperatives in the region.

Kibbutzim and collective moshavim are production cooperatives and as such are without many parallels in the developed Western countries. Moshavim and secondary regional cooperatives, on the other hand, are similar in their purchasing, marketing, and primary processing functions to multipurpose and requisite cooperatives in the U.K. and regional cooperatives in the U.S. However, in Israel one of the major functions of agricultural cooperatives is raising credit for their members – a function normally reserved in Western countries to specialized cooperative banking institutions.

Financial cooperation has developed into one of the major functions of all agricultural cooperatives in Israel because nationally owned land cannot be used as collateral for borrowing. Instead of land, security is provided by the pooled production resources of the members who are all mutually liable for the debt of the cooperative.

Credit intermediation under the umbrella of mutual liability was all pervasive in Israeli agriculture until the crisis. Kibbutzim in law represent their members to the banks and raise money centrally. Farmers on a moshav, unlike kibbutz members, have individual financial needs, yet usually they did not apply directly to the bank for a loan: they borrowed all the money that they needed from their primary cooperative, the moshav association, which expected to recover the loans from produce marketing revenues through interlinkage agreements with the members. The moshav association, in turn, raised money from the banks on the strength of mutual guarantees of the moshav members or went straight to its secondary regional cooperative – the purchasing organization – for more loans. The purchasing organization relied on a much broader base of mutual guarantees provided by all its primary member cooperatives in its financial dealings with banks and suppliers. The credit raised by the purchasing organization was normally channeled to its members the moshavim or regional enterprises – in back-to-back arrangements. Mutual liability in effect provided a risk pooling mechanism which was one of the main advantages of financial cooperation in Israel (Zusman 1988).

1.2. Development of Agricultural Debt

Israeli agriculture, with its advanced technology and high capital intensity, needs continued infusion of funds to finance investments and working capital. While industrial and commercial firms can raise equity capital by selling stock to external investors, the small family firms in agriculture are restricted to equity formation through retained earnings, which are the residual component of farm profits and private consumption and are therefore not always sufficient. The large agricultural bodies in Israel, such as kibbutzim and regional enterprises, in principle could attract outside investors, but being organized as cooperatives their principal function is to serve their members and they are not geared to accommodate external shareholders. Cooperatives are moreover forbidden in law to issue stock to nonmembers. Israeli cooperatives, similarly to many agricultural cooperatives in the world, are thus forced to rely mainly on debt as a source of financing their growth. Neglect of equity financing was further encouraged by government investment and development support policies, which often made it possible to finance new assets with what seemed, at least on paper, like "more than one hundred percent debt".

Agriculture has enjoyed (at least in the last two decades) a generous supply of credit. From 1969 to 1987, the outstanding agricultural debt from banks increased by a factor of 6.5 in constant domestic prices (Figure 1.1). By comparison, the manufacturing industries increased their outstanding debt only by a factor of 4 in the same period. It is remarkable that agricultural debt began outstripping the industrial debt only in 1980, when reforms in securities regulation encouraged industrial and commercial corporations to turn aggressively to raising equity in the stock exchange, while agriculture was forced to continue relying almost totally on debt.

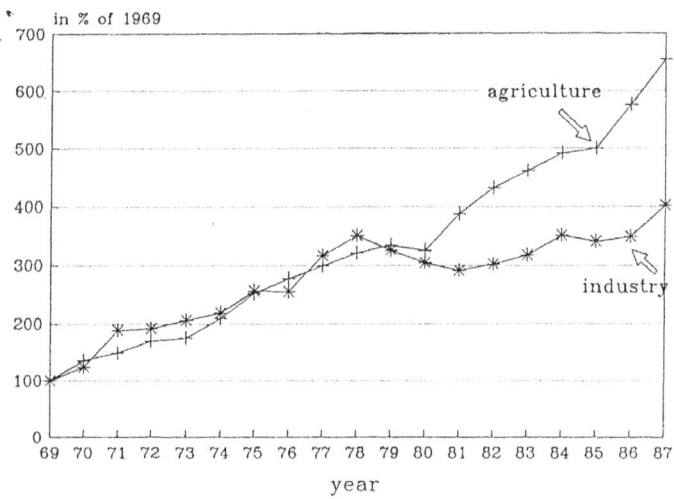

Figure 1.1. Growth of real bank credit in Israeli agriculture and industry, 1969-1987.

Agricultural debt also increased more than in other sectors in relation to product and to capital stock. Table 1.2 shows that the financial leverage (the ratio of debt to production assets) increased by a factor of 4.2 in agriculture between 1969 and 1986 and merely by 23 percent in manufacturing industries. The ratio of agricultural debt to output increased by a factor of

3.8 in the same period, while ratio of debt to gross national product for the economy as a whole increased only by a factor of 2.2.

Agriculture enjoys a variety of sources for borrowing. It is estimated that only about one fifth of total agricultural debt is commercial bank credit: the rest, although channeled for technical reasons through the banking system, derives from government-directed sources. These include funds from government development budget, Jewish Agency settlement budget, investment grants and loans, directed export-assistance loans, and earmarked loans for specific designated uses. The pervasive government involvement in agricultural financing is an historical continuation of the traditional view of agriculture as the main objective of Zionism – settlement of penniless Jewish immigrants repatriated from all points of the compass to their national home.

TABLE 1.2: Ratio of Outstanding Debt to Gross Product and Net Capital (selected years, end of year data, real values)

Year	Total credit, % of GNP	Credit to agriculture, % of agricultural product	Credit to agriculture	Credit to industry
			% of net capital	
1969	30.8	47.6	18.8	51.7
1974	48.3	75.9	34.9	69.2
1979	57.2	100.9	47.9	75.1
1984	57.3	177.0	67.3	69.6
1988	66.8	182.3	79.4	63.5

Source: Credit balance from Bank of Israel, Inspector of Bank, *Annual Bank Statistics*, various issues; GNP and agricultural product from Israel Central Statistics Bureau, *Statistical Abstract of Israel*, various issues; capital stock data from Buck (1984) and privately communicated updates.

Unlike physical inputs, whose free supply and demand are only limited by market prices, credit is rationed, so that increased availability of credit to some sectors or clienteles is in itself a bonus. In addition to increasing the supply of credit to selected users, the government may subsidize the cost of credit either by charging a concessionary, below-market interest rate or by distributing part of the funds in the form of grants. Table 1.3 shows that the real annual cost of government development loans in 1979 was negative, minus 29 percent (after adjusting the nominal rate for ex-post inflation in that year). At the end of 1970s, the development loans were indexed, which of course substantially reduced the subsidy component, yet the cost of indexed development loans still remained below the market rates. Short-term directed loans for export uses remained unindexed, and the negative effective real cost of this credit component persisted for a longer time. The availability of directed loans to agriculture has been severely reduced in recent years, however.

The cost of free credit in Table 1.3 represents mainly the cost of overdraft facilities in commercial banks. It is influenced by the attempts of the banks to set nominal interest rates that compensate for the expected (ex-ante) inflation. These attempts, of course, were doomed to failure in the Israeli environment with its very high and highly variable inflation rates. As a consequence, the real (inflation-adjusted) bank rates were low and even negative in some periods, while in other period they were positive and even usuriously high. Following the severe anti-inflationary measures instituted by the government in 1985, that brought the annual inflation rates down from 400 percent annualized in the first half of 1985 to 100 percent annualized in the second half and to 20 percent in 1986, the banks reduced the nominal interest rates dramatically. This reduction, however, lagged far behind the decrease in inflation rates, so that the real cost of debt skyrocketed. The combination of anti-inflationary economic policy with natural stickiness of interest rates in fact triggered the financial crisis in agriculture.

TABLE 1.3: Real Annual Cost of Debt (in percent)

Year	Overdraft and free credit	Short-term directed credit	Industrial investment loans
1979	−11	−45	−26.0
1981	34	−28	−6.0
1983	−3	−44	0.5
1985	100	−23	2.5
1986	31	−3	1.6
1987	0.9	3	0.9

Source: *Bank of Israel Report*, various years.
Note: The data are for credit to all sectors of the economy: no separate data for agricultural credit are available. Sample data show that the cost of agricultural credit was in line with the rest of the economy.

The generous subsidies to various sources of credit have encouraged borrowing and financing of physical assets with debt. As a result, the capital intensity of agriculture, or the capital stock per person employed in agriculture, increased. Yet subsidies and extensive reliance on debt financing are risky propositions: if the outstanding debt is high, unanticipated external changes in interest rates may raise the financing charges to such an extent that the debtor will be unable to service the debt. This danger is particularly acute in situations when long-term investments are financed with short-term loans that require frequent rollover at the new, increased rates, as was often the case in Israeli agriculture. An extreme case illustrating these risks and dangers is indeed provided by the recent financial crisis.

Israeli agriculture has weathered similar crises in the past (although admittedly of smaller magnitude) . Throughout the past crises, the government and other public bodies invariably intervened by rescheduling the agricultural debt to longer terms and reducing the cost of debt. This phenomenon became known as "conversion" in Israeli economic parlance, and the almost predictable recurrence of "conversions"· (sometimes every two or three years in different segments of agriculture) has created an implied understanding in the agricultural sector and in the banking community that the government and the public sector were committed to rescuing or bailing out the agriculture in case of financial difficulties.

Aware of its implicit commitment, the government sought ways to break the vicious circle of overborrowing and "conversions" by increasing its involvement in the decision-making process preliminary to borrowing and in the monitoring of the uses of funds. The "concentrated credit" scheme was implemented in the early 1960s, whereby each agricultural village, a moshav or a kibbutz, was assigned to a "central" commercial bank that was responsible for its financing needs and in return was given the power, together with a committee of government and public sector representatives, of vetting all investment proposals. The scheme was voluntary, and the inducement for joining was easier availability of credit at better terms. Most of the agricultural villages indeed joined the "concentrated credit" scheme during the first few years after its implementation. However, the carefully designed scheme broke down in the 1970s, as the availability of free bank credit in Israel increased and the terms offered by "concentrated credit" lost their advantage. It was at that period that the regional "purchasing organizations" began developing their financial intermediation activities, freely borrowing from the banks and making the loans available back-to-back to their member cooperatives. This naturally led to the demise of "concentrated credit" with its well-intentioned plans for control and monitoring of agricultural spending.

1.3. Financial Crisis

The financial crisis was triggered in 1985/86 by the abrupt increase in real interest rates of short-term bank credit. The farmers and their cooperatives could not continue servicing the debt at the new rates and the creditors responded by refusing to roll over the short-term loans. Many purchasing cooperatives were forced to stop their routine input purchasing activities, the production in regional enterprises was crippled by financing shortages, and services to many villages were stopped.

When farmers and cooperatives ceased making interest payments on outstanding loans, the banks began accruing the interest charges calculated at the abnormally high rights, adding them periodically to the unpaid principal. This is the source of most of the rapid increase in outstanding bank debt in 1986 and 1987 that we witness in Figure 1.1: there was very little new agricultural borrowing at that time and the debt burden continued increasing through accrual of unpaid interest.

Although the abnormally high interest rates triggered the crisis, its origins were much more fundamental. As we have noted previously, nearly 80 percent of agricultural debt was subsidized in various degrees. This, and persistent delays in the adjustment of interest rates to inflation, resulted in persistently low real average cost of all outstanding agricultural debt up to 1984. In a sample of moshavim and regional cooperatives, the ex post real cost of debt in 1983-84 was found to be lower than minus 30 percent annually (Figure 1.2).

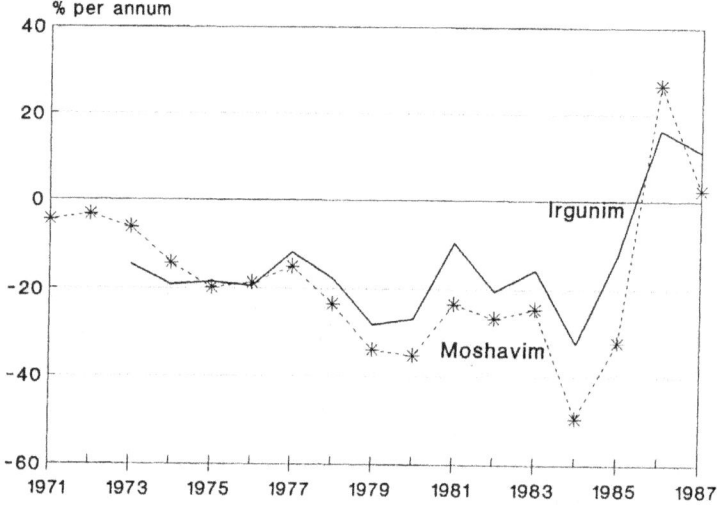

Figure 1.2. Real cost of outstanding debt: averages for four supply cooperatives and four moshavim.

Negative interest rates imply erosion of principal and provide an opportunity for equity formation in the form of holding gains. However, agriculture failed to build its equity base during this inflationary period. On the contrary, the financial leverage of agriculture – the ratio of outstanding debt to net assets – steadily increased to 0.67 in 1984 and continued increasing as debt levels grew (see Table 1.2).

Chronically cheap debt encouraged overborrowing which, at least in part, was applied to finance new productive assets. The result was over-investment, leading to low efficiency of the capital employed and increased risk. Heavy reliance on debt is manifested in heavy interest payments that must be made out of current cash earnings. The relatively high variability of agricultural earnings may lead to temporary or recurrent inability to meet the interest payments if these exceed certain prudent levels. Moreover, the covariance of different agricultural enterprises is relatively high, because the states of nature are the same for all farmers, so that all segments of agriculture are likely to be unable to pay the finance charges at roughly the same time. The covariance was particularly high in Israeli cooperative agriculture, where, say, the bank loans held by purchasing organizations were secured by the assets of the member moshavim, which in turn were accounts receivable from the farmers in these moshavim. When the farmers at the bottom of the pyramid woke up to the fact that their earnings in 1985/86 were insufficient to pay the interest charges, the shock spread through the entire system as a domino effect resulting at the top in technical default of the entire agricultural sector. Mutual liability, which provided an effective risk pooling device in normal times and encouraged borrowing, failed when all members of the system, through their high covariances, defaulted simultaneously.

With such high and steadily increasing levels of debt relative to capital assets and output, a crisis was unavoidable sooner or later. If not triggered by a change in interest rates, it would have been triggered by a deterioration of terms of trade or an increase in labor costs, say. The fact that high interest rates provided the specific trigger exacerbated the situation, because the outstanding debt continued to swell due to the accrual of financing charges, but other trigger factors could have equally exposed the deficient capital structure of agriculture and precipitated a financial crisis.

The prevailing impression since 1985/86 is that we are facing a financial crisis of the cooperative agricultural sector. The diverse and rich data collected by several public committees since the eruption of the crisis reflect mainly the state of cooperative agriculture – kibbutzim, moshavim, and their regional cooperatives. Relatively little data are available for the 20 percent of Israeli agriculture represented by private Jewish and Arab farmers. The feeling is that private agriculture, although definitely under financial stress, is in a much better shape than cooperative agriculture. Some segments of cooperative agriculture also appear to be doing better than others. For instance, the small Orthodox Religious Kibbutz Movement remains unscathed and there are regional cooperatives that continue operating safely and profitably. Despite these differences, however, the overall sense is that of a debt crisis in cooperative agriculture. Why in the cooperative sector in particular?

When a business firm runs into financial distress, the creditors have two options: (a) to liquidate the firm's assets in order to recover, at least in part, their investment or (b) to assist the firm until it regains profitability and resumes orderly debt service. The first option is irrelevant when an entire sector of the economy is in financial distress: who will buy the assets of Israeli agriculture from the banks and other creditors? The only solution is restoration of the sector's ability to repay its debt in the long run. Various rehabilitation schemes have been proposed, involving a joint effort of the government, the banks, and the cooperatives. The basic components of these schemes are essentially rescheduling of debt to a longer term (in the "conversion" tradition) , retroactive reduction of interest rates to reasonable levels, and partial forgiveness. The government plays a dual role in these schemes: it bears part of the cost (roughly one third of the forgiven debt) but, more importantly, it acts as a mediator bringing the banks and the cooperatives to a negotiating table in order to avoid a dangerous stalemate and to resolve the crisis with the objective of resuming normal operations in the agricultural sector.

There are interesting parallels between the debt crisis of cooperative agriculture in Israel and the recent LDC debt crisis, especially in Latin American countries. The similarity starts at the root of the problem: recycling of petrodollars in mid-1970s. In an attempt to find productive and seemingly profitable uses to the oil producers' surpluses, the major banks were willing to make loans to the less developed weak countries. The influx of foreign loans, followed by conspicuous investment projects and public expenditure, created a feeling of prosperity and economic success in the debtor countries. The banks continued lending on the promise of this success, until the bubble exploded in the early 1980s. The debtor and creditor nations negotiated for more than a decade. The capital flows were reversed, from poor to rich countries. The banks lost part of their investment (the outstanding debt was discounted up to 90 percent), but no satisfactory agreements have been worked out.

In Israel, the abundant supply of credit also originated partly from foreign sources, in the years when the world credit supply was expanding. And just as it was inconceivable that the major banks would "liquidate" the less-developed debtor nations in order to recover their money, so was it unthinkable that the whole agricultural sector in Israel would be sold off to the highest bidder in order to repay its debt to the banks. In the international arena, debtor nations relied on supranational bodies – the World Bank and the International Monetary Fund – to work out compromise agreements. In Israel, the active involvement of the government in these negotiations at least produced an agreement, although a long way remained to its successful implementation.

Unfortunately, the external shock produced by Israel's 1985 anti-inflationary policy, with its credit squeeze and dramatic increase in interest rates, combined with deteriorating terms of trade and declining profitability of agriculture. Moreover, comparison of the changes in output to uses of current inputs and capital assets indicates that farmers failed to anticipate the decline in earnings. Investments and expansion of capacity continued, increasing the debt burden, while revenues stagnated and operating profits turned to losses before allowing for interest charges. The result was financial disaster, because agriculture in the second half of the 1980s did not have the earning power to pay the very high financing charges calculated at the new, much increased interest rates on the large volume of debt accumulated in previous periods. The financial crisis struck in a sector that, on the one hand, was characterized by over-capacity financed with overborrowing and, on the other, by severely diminished earning power.

1.4. Financial Cooperation

Financial cooperation has always been a cornerstone of cooperative agriculture in Israel. Purchasing organizations and moshav associations acted as financial intermediaries channeling loan funds between the banks and their members. These cooperatives also acted as clearinghouses: farmers would deposit surplus cash in their moshav association, which would use these deposits to lend to cash-short members. Moshavim and kibbutzim with surplus cash would similarly deposit it in regional cooperatives, which would then lend these funds to other member villages. The mutual aid in regional cooperatives and in moshavim was mainly in the form of financial assistance: making credit available to members to bridge over transient needs.

The farmers in cooperative agriculture do not own their land: it is leased to them by the state through the moshav association. Other attached rights, such as production quotas and water rights, are not the farmers' property either: the rights are allocated to the moshav association, which distributes them to the members. These rights are not transferable and not tradeable. Moshav farms can be sold, with "rights on", but only on condition that the buyer is admitted as a new member in the moshav association. Banks cannot foreclose on farms and agricultural land in case of default, and the farmers' inability to use these assets as collateral was one of the main reasons for the development of cooperative credit institutions in Israel – moshav associations for farmers and regional purchasing organizations for kibbutzim and moshavim.

The depth of credit cooperation in Israeli agriculture is clearly seen from Table 1.4, which shows summary balance sheets of a purchasing organization and a representative moshav from the same region. The moshav balance sheet shows only the association's assets, which do not include the members' farm assets. More than three quarters of the association' s assets are loans to moshav members. These are mostly short-term loans on open account ("accounts receivable from members"), which are only secured by marketing interlinkage agreement: the member undertakes to market his farm produce centrally through the moshav association, so that the sales revenues collected by the association will be used to repay the current loan. The principal source of funds for the moshav association are loans from the purchasing organization (76.9 percent) and members' deposits (13.5 percent). The moshav association thus acts as a clearinghouse among members and as a financial intermediary between the members and an outside institution – the regional purchasing organization.

In the purchasing organization, over 60 percent of assets are receivables from member moshavim and 18.3 percent are loans to regional service enterprises owned by the purchasing organization and the moshavim in the region. Loan funds to member cooperatives were raised by borrowing from outside creditors (banks and others) and by a hefty suppliers' credit. Some purchasing organizations (although not the one in Table 1.4) also acted as clearinghouses, accepting deposits from moshavim and regional enterprises with surplus cash.

TABLE 1.4: Balance Sheet Composition of a Moshav Association and a Regional Supply Cooperative, September 30, 1981 (in percent of total assets)

ASSETS	Moshav	Supply coop	LIABILITIES	Moshav	Supply coop
Fixed assets	3.7	3.5	Equity	0.7	3.0
Long-term investments and loans to members	3.5	13.7	Long-term debt	4.2	19.5
Inventories	4.0	--	Short-term loans from banks	0.6	34.5
Accounts receivable			Short-term loans		
Non-members	12.2	3.6	from supply	76.9	--
Regional enterprises	--	18.3	cooperative		
			Suppliers' credit	4.1	21.8
Members' debit balances	76.6	60.9	Members' credit balances	13.5	21.2
Total	100.0	100.0	Total	100.0	100.0

In a kibbutz, the members' activities are part of the cooperative effort. The kibbutz is obliged to supply all members' needs, and, unlike moshav members, kibbutz members do not borrow from their cooperative. Receivables from members are therefore conspicuously absent from all kibbutz balance sheets. Yet kibbutzim, similarly to moshav associations, rely on cooperative borrowing from their regional purchasing organizations and from similar facilities established by the national kibbutz movements. The component of direct borrowing from banks, however, is more pronounced in kibbutzim than in moshav associations, because of the broader production activities of kibbutzim.

Advantages

As noted above, one of the main reasons for the development of cooperative credit was the lack of collateral in Israeli agriculture. Mutual liability developed as a substitute for standard collateral: moshav members jointly guaranteed the loans of their village association, moshavim and kibbutzim jointly guaranteed the loans of their regional purchasing associations, kibbutzim guaranteed the loans of their national movements which, in turn, guaranteed the direct loans of the kibbutzim from commercial banks. Mutual liability was regarded as an excellent risk pooling mechanism for both creditors and members: the creditors were secured by the combined income-generating capacity of all the "mutual guarantors", while individual members and cooperatives could count on mutual liability to help smooth out the variability of their earnings streams, which otherwise could prove stressful.

The mutual liability evolved, probably unintentionally and unconsciously, into an all-encompassing and unlimited guarantee. It has never been limited to specific amounts or to specific events. Yet the banks placed their trust in this mechanism: a mutual liability rider was usually required as a precondition of borrowing by an agricultural cooperative. Yet when the crunch came, mutual liability failed to come up to its expectations.

The perception of mutual liability as a risk pooling mechanism increased the availability of credit to agricultural cooperatives. Farmers and their cooperatives always had the option of approaching the banks directly for loans. Yet without proper collateral their borrowing capacity would be restricted and the cost of debt probably would be higher.

In addition to increasing the availability of credit, financial cooperation had other advantages also: mutual liability arrangements induced explicit and implicit peer monitoring, creating social pressures to comply with cooperative norms and thus reducing the likelihood that an individual farmer or an individual cooperative will default on outstanding obligation; marketing interlinkage arrangements, in addition to securing the repayment of members' debt to the moshav association, also provided the association with detailed information for predicting and monitoring its future cash flows and thus negotiating bank loans at the best possible terms; finally, the concentration of financial activities increased the level of professional financial management available to individual farmers.

Weaknesses

Yet financial cooperation also suffers from distinct weaknesses. Providing as it does a kind of an insurance policy against individual failure, mutual liability may enhance the manifestations of mutual hazard in cooperatives: members and associations may tend to undertake excessively risky investments and to over-invest in general on the strength of the belief that they will not bear the entire cost of failure if the investment project underperforms. Free riders may bypass the marketing interlinkage agreements and sell their produce individually outside the cooperative system, thus depriving the cooperative of the repayment security on its loans, weakening the association's financial standing, and ultimately restricting the access of all other members to credit sources. As a result of differences in horizon preferences, some members may support policies favoring short-term gains at the expense of long-term performance in the expectation that they will exit in the long run, leaving all the remaining members to shoulder the accumulated liabilities. Finally, mutual liability is not free from agency costs: although banks may regard the cooperatives as their agents, entrusted with the duty of overseeing the orderly repayment of the loans under the mutual liability umbrella (by limiting credit to insolvent farms, say), the cooperatives are guided by their own interests which are not necessarily identical to those of the creditors.

Accountability causes particular difficulties in cooperatives: the democratic management of cooperatives is largely based on the "buddy system", where all officers and members are personal acquaintances, not to say friends. This counteracts peer monitoring in the sense that the decisions of cooperative managers are often accepted without searching questions and there is little outside control of management decisions.

Political pressures in the democratically elected cooperative may result in insufficient enforcement. An incumbent manager may find it difficult to refuse a request for more credit from a member whom he knows to be insolvent or a free rider because strict enforcement may cost the manager the member's vote in the next election. Enforcement difficulties are actually reflected in the behavior of moshav members. A rough measure of the financial exposure of a member is the ratio of outstanding debt to monthly sales through the cooperative ("credit-months"). During the period 1977-1981, 13 of the 24 moshavim in the regional supply cooperative of Table 1.4 exceeded 12 credit-months for relatively long durations (Zusman 1988). Moshavim with 55 and 42 credit-months were observed in another supply cooperative (Kislev and Marvid 1988). More than a few farm operators owe their moshav associations several times their annual production capacity. Moshavim or farmers with such heavy debt burdens relative to their production capacity will never be able to repay their loans. Liabilities amounting to dozens of credit-months testify to weakness of control and enforcement in cooperatives, weakness that breeds permissiveness and lax financial discipline.

Financial cooperation with its adjuncts of mutual liability and marketing interlinkage appeared to function successfully and effectively for decades. Yet at a certain point in time it began to be abused through moral hazard, free riding, lack of accountability, and insufficient enforcement. These weaknesses of financial cooperation were among the reasons for the 1985/86 financial crisis in agriculture. Regional service enterprises provide a good capsule case of the cumulative effect of these weaknesses.

1.5. Regional Enterprises

Regional service enterprises were ordinarily organized as limited liability cooperative associations and their establishment was largely financed by government investment grants and subsidized loans. Their membership consisted of kibbutzim and moshavim, mostly potential patrons of the service offered. Often the regional supply coop was also a member and in all cases it provided the enterprises in the region with short term financing and purchasing services.

Zealous pursuit of rural development by public agencies, easy access to credit through the supply cooperatives, and strong political regional lobbies resulted in over-expansion of the service enterprises. These trends were particularly prevalent in the 1970s, when credit was in ample supply and economic optimism ran high. Not unlike firms in a cartel, regionals scrambled to grab their share in the service enterprises, with all the expected ensuing benefits. Consequently, in the early 1980s many service enterprises operated under capacity: 50-60 percent by the estimate of the State Controller. The final outcome was that many of the enterprises could not even cover their operating costs.

Strong economic relations developed between the two kinds of regionals – the supply coop and the service enterprises – a relationship that proved detrimental when the financial crisis erupted at the end of 1985. Particularly detrimental was the establishment of ownership relations between supply cooperatives and regional enterprises in the moshav subsector. While all regional enterprises in the kibbutz subsector were always and still are owned by the member-kibbutzim, i.e., directly by the users, the balance of wealth in the moshav subsector was such that cash-rich supply cooperatives were allowed to establish and own various regional service enterprises, to be used by their member-moshavim. The separation of the regional enterprises from ownership by direct users apparently exacerbated the weaknesses of cooperative organization discussed above.

The supply cooperatives, assuming the role of the financiers of last resort, found themselves financing not only operating losses but also the debt service of the regional enterprises. Already in 1981, the share of credit to the service enterprises in the assets of the supply coop in Table 1.4 was 18.3 percent; it grew substantially thereafter. In one case (Kislev and Marvid 1988) it was found that a regional slaughterhouse that started operation in 1981 with equity representing 25 percent of its inflation adjusted capital began accumulating losses and by 1985 its debt reached 2.5 times the value of its assets, most of that short term loans from the supply coop. This was an extreme case but not atypical; when the service enterprises began failing in 1985, they took many of the supply coops down with them.

Most of the regional enterprises in the moshav subsector went into liquidation following the 1986 financial crisis in agriculture. Most of the regional enterprises in the kibbutz subsector survived and continue operating with varying degrees of profitability and success. It is for this reason that the Israeli sample for this research consists entirely of regional enterprises owned and used by kibbutzim.

2. Implications of the Theory of Cooperative Behavior for Performance Evaluation of Cooperatives

Cooperatives are regarded as a separate form of business organization, extending the conventional classification of single proprietorships, partnerships, and investor-owned firms (IOFs). Cooperatives operate in the same economic environment with IOFs, buying, selling, and producing goods and services. Unlike IOFs, however, cooperatives aim to provide a service to their member patrons rather than earn a return on an investment; cooperatives distribute profits or surpluses according to patronage and not according to investment. In addition to their business activity, cooperatives also provide goods and services for which no market values are available: they are active incommunity development, member education, government lobbying on behalf of members, and are often regarded as providing a training ground for participatory management and democratic governance. The specific features of the cooperative form of organization are sufficiently distinctive to suggest that cooperatives may pursue different objectives from IOFs. The issue addressed in this research is whether the difference in objectives between cooperatives and investor-owned firms outweighs the effect of the similarities in business functions.

The difference in objectives may be attributable to the origin of cooperatives. In market economies, groups of producers or consumers have formed cooperatives when they became dissatisfied with the conduct of investor-owned firms. Cooperatives have thus been viewed as a tool for correcting market failures (Schrader 1989a), such as those found in the agricultural sector with its thin and spatially distributed markets. Indeed, Nourse (1922), in his concept of cooperatives as a competitive yardstick, felt cooperatives should exist in order to eliminate monopolistic excesses of profit-oriented firms.

According to a survey performed by Purdue University in the late 1970s and early 1980s (Schrader et al. 1985), policy makers and university economists were reported to feel that there were significant differences between the goals of cooperatives and investor-owned firms and that these differences in goals caused differences in business strategy. On the other hand, as part of the same survey, Babb and Lang (1985) found that managers of cooperatives and proprietary firms ranked their goals essentially the same. Perhaps this difference in opinion between "theoreticians" and "practitioners" is due to the absence of generally accepted performance criteria for cooperatives, which may be caused by disagreements over the role or function of cooperatives in society.

2.1. Theoretical Basis for the Comparison of Cooperatives and IOFs

Cooperatives are a form of collective action in which individuals join together to accomplish what would be costlier or impossible to achieve individually (Zusman 1988). Farmers and other small operators, for example, have formed cooperatives to ameliorate their disadvantage in the market system. Yet economists and managers frequently view cooperatives simply as a variant of an investor-owned firm, modeling them with an objective function that reflects the specific features of cooperative organization (Staatz 1989). For example, an appropriate objective function of a cooperative, as originally suggested by Enke (1945), may be to maximize the sum of producer surplus (profits) and consumer surplus (lower prices). Cooperatives also have been modeled as having a zero-profit objective and as maximizing average per unit surplus or price received by members (Helmberger and Hoos 1962).

While conceptual frameworks for a more comprehensive analysis of cooperative performance are suggested later at the end of this chapter, cooperatives are viewed in this research as a variant of investor-owned firms (IOFs) and their performance is evaluated by standard business measures developed for IOFs. If in this setting cooperative performance is found to be inferior to IOF performance, it can be argued that the result is biased downward because of the additional member welfare dimensions in cooperatives that are not captured by standard business performance measures. Yet if cooperative performance as evaluated by standard business measures is found to be not "worse" than IOF performance, there is a reason to suggest that the overall benefits enjoyed by cooperative members may exceed the benefits of IOF shareholders.

The theory of cooperatives and the accepted views of cooperative behavior suggest fundamental differences in objectives and business strategy between cooperatives and IOFs, which are basically traceable to differences in ownership structure of the two categories of organizations. These differences should lead to observable differences in capital structure, profitability, and operating efficiency of cooperatives and IOFs, which can be estimated by standard measures of financial performance evaluation originally developed for IOFs, such as financial ratio analysis.

Ownership Structure and the Role of Equity Capital in Cooperatives

Cooperatives are user-owned firms: owners are at the same time the patrons. The ownership structure of cooperatives is thus different from that of the conventional firm, which transacts business with clienteles that are typically separated from the investors who own the firm. Investors in conventional firms (i.e., IOFs) receive a return proportional to their investment, and IOFs are therefore driven to maximize earnings adjusted for risk in the interest of the owners. Investors in cooperatives, on the other hand, expect to receive direct benefits through doing business with the cooperative rather than earn a return on their invested capital. It can be argued that members' interests are not necessarily best served by maximizing the earnings of the cooperative: better results for the member-owners may be achieved by reducing the charges they pay for the services provided by the cooperative or increasing the prices they receive for the products marketed through the cooperative (Staatz 1989), although both strategies inevitably reduce cooperative earnings.

The difference in objectives between cooperatives and IOFs stemming from the dissimilarity in ownership structure suggests a number of distinctions in business and financial strategy of cooperatives (Condon 1987; Cotterill 1987; LeVay 1983; Staatz, 1987). One of the main differences is that cooperative equity, unlike IOF stock, is not marketable. Non-patrons have no motivation to invest in a cooperative, because the distribution of cooperative earnings is based on patronage, and not investment. As a result, there are no secondary markets for cooperative stock, and cooperatives are restricted to raising equity from member-producers who use the services of the cooperative (Condon and Vitaliano 1983; Staatz, 1989).

Because of the non-marketability of cooperative stock, members may be reluctant to increase their illiquid equity stake in the cooperative. Indeed, Royer (1985) reports that direct infusion of equity by members accounts for less than 15 percent of the increase in the equity base of the 100 largest cooperatives from 1980-1984. Members may also be reluctant to allow the cooperative to increase its equity base through retained earnings, because retention of earnings translates into lower effective prices for marketed products or higher effective costs of farm inputs. In contrast, shareholders in IOFs are indifferent, at least in theory, between cash distributions and retained earnings, because the latter translate into market appreciation of equity, which can be realized by investors through selling their shares in the secondary market (Brealey and Myers 1991; Copeland and Weston 1983).

Faced with such fundamental restrictions on accumulation of equity capital, many cooperatives have developed a system whereby part of the earnings are retained in the form of allocated patronage refunds, which are redeemed, i.e., paid out in cash to members, with a lag of several years (Cobia et al. 1982). This system partly alleviates the members' liquidity constraints caused by non-marketability of cooperative stock and at the same time provides the cooperative with an important source of equity capital for growth: the top 100 cooperatives have on average 50 percent of their equity in the form of allocated retained earnings (Kane 1988). Unlike the traditional permanent equity, however, the allocated patronage refunds are in the nature of "deferred dividends" or "interest free loans" (depending on the bias of the financial analyst), and the cooperative is forced to generate enough earnings to finance periodic equity redemption in addition to financing its growth.

However, these equity retention systems in cooperatives are basically an analog of accumulation of equity from retained earnings in IOFs: they cannot replace the other source of equity available to IOFs, namely raising equity through new stock issues. Despite the promise of ultimate redemption of allocated patronage refunds, cooperatives probably cannot abuse this mechanism by relying on it to satisfy all their equity needs. The potential danger of "equity starvation" in a cooperative thus remains.

Capital Structure

Corporations in most cases cannot finance their operations and growth only with internally generated funds and require external financing in the form of new equity issues or debt. The higher the proportion of debt in a firm's capital structure, the greater are the risks associated with the probability of default, while lower leverage generally indicates greater financial security. With respect to capital structure, at least two factors suggest that cooperatives can be expected to have a higher proportion of debt than comparable IOFs.

First, as noted above, cooperatives are frequently viewed as "equity bound": cooperative stock is not an attractive investment because it provides no opportunity for increased value through earnings and because there are limitations on dividends, voting rights, and transfer of shares. As a result, there is no secondary market for cooperative stock (Staatz 1989), which restricts the opportunities for raising equity from both nonmembers and members. While IOFs can distribute their financing needs between raising new debt and issuing new equity, cooperatives are believed to be much more constrained in their ability to raise equity. The anticipated shortage of equity in cooperatives is expected to influence their growth and financing decisions (Schrader 1989b). Cooperatives can compensate for the theoretically expected shortage of equity capital by financing a relatively high portion of their growth with debt. Cooperatives therefore may need to rely more heavily on debt financing than IOFs in order to sustain comparable growth rates.

Second, cooperatives and IOFs may differ in their attitudes toward risk. The cooperative principle of risk sharing and mutual responsibility may be interpreted by cooperative managers as providing an "insurance policy" in case of adverse business outcomes (Zusman 1988). Recent findings suggest that a merger with a financially strong cooperative is the preferred alternative to bankruptcy for failing cooperatives – over 70 percent of the mergers among agricultural cooperatives in Minnesota in 1979-84 involved a partner in a net loss position (Parliament and Taitt 1989), in contrast to only 6 percent of the mergers among IOFs in a national study (Ravenscraft and Scherer 1987). Thus, unlike the shareholders of an IOF, which are often the main losers when the firm is dissolved, the members in a failing cooperative will not necessarily suffer, because they will continue to receive essentially the same services from the acquiring cooperative. This sense of "insurance" mitigating the ultimate outcome of failure may cause cooperative decision makers to display moral hazard behavior, which should manifest itself in willingness to assume higher levels of risk than the managers of "uninsured" investor-owned firms. Cooperatives thus can be expected to borrow more heavily than IOFs and have lower safety margins against the risk of default.

Profitability

With respect to profitability, cooperatives, in contrast to IOFs, are seldom regarded as rate-of-return maximizers: cooperative members expect to receive benefits through services provided by the cooperative, such as lower input prices or better marketing channels, and not through a direct return on their investment in cooperative equity (Staatz 1989). The service benefits that members receive from their cooperative reduce the reported revenues and increase the reported costs, so that cooperatives can be expected to show lower reported profitability than IOFs.

In the traditional model of a cooperative as a firm with zero-profit objective (Helmberger and Hoos 1962), prices and charges are adjusted so that no surplus is generated. Zero profit, while highly undesirable for IOFs, should not be particularly harmful to cooperatives: the members of a zero-profit cooperative may still be receiving their payoff in the form of higher product prices or lower costs. Moreover, cooperative members may treat profits with indifference, because they rely on being able to get back their investment after a certain number of years through equity redemption schemes (Cobia et al. 1982) and do not necessarily expect to earn a rate of return on their investment.

Operating Efficiency

With respect to operating efficiency, as measured by the utilization of assets to generate sales, moral hazard considerations also suggest that cooperatives may be less discriminating in undertaking investments than IOFs. Thus, cooperatives may have a tendency to "overinvest," forming an asset base greater than the asset base of IOFs for the same level of sales. "Over-investment" on the part of cooperatives may also arise from differences in the evaluation of the opportunity cost of equity funds. Because members usually do not expect a direct return on their investment in the cooperative and rely on long-term equity redemption schemes, cooperatives may treat members' equity as costless funds, without acknowledging their opportunity cost. This, of course, is totally inconsistent with the actual risk exposure of equity funds in any corporation and even more so with the need for "capital rationing" that may be imposed by the scarcity of equity in cooperatives.

Undervaluing the cost of equity, combined with higher propensity to borrow due to susceptibility to moral hazard behavior in cooperatives, may encourage excessive investments, leading to lower efficiency of asset utilization and higher asset growth rates for cooperatives than for IOFs. Overinvestment need not be restricted to fixed assets: it can also affect current assets, resulting in higher levels of inventory for a given level of sales.

It is sometimes claimed that undervaluation of members' equity should result in too much equity funds relative to debt in the capital structure of cooperatives, contrary of the expectation of higher leverage due to moral hazard behavior. This could indeed be so if cooperatives were to restrict their growth to rates supportable by the relatively limited opportunities of raising such "costless" equity. However, at growth rates at least comparable to the rest of the industry, "equity bound" cooperatives will be forced to borrow more than comparable IOFs.

2.2. Operationalization of the Hypotheses

The various hypotheses suggested by the theory of cooperative behavior can be tested by analyzing standard financial ratios for cooperatives and

IOFs. The attitude of cooperatives toward return on members' investment can be deduced by comparative examination of the rate of return to equity. The argument that cooperatives are likely to carry higher debt levels than IOFs because they are "equity bound" and susceptible to moral hazard behavior can be tested by a comparative examination of the debt to equity ratio. The implications of moral hazard behavior, suggesting willingness to assume higher levels of risk, can also be tested by comparing the solvency and liquidity of cooperatives and IOFs, as measured respectively by the ratio of earnings to interest payments and by the ratio of current assets to current liabilities. The claim that cooperatives tend to "overinvest" can be tested by comparing the ratio of sales to fixed assets and the asset growth rates in cooperatives and IOFs. Comparison of inventory turnover ratios provides a test of overinvestment in current assets.

The profitability, capital structure, and operating efficiency ratios used in this research are defined in Table 2.1. The table also indicates the expected relationships of these ratios for cooperatives and IOFs based on the previous discussion of the theory of cooperative behavior.

TABLE 2.1: Standard Financial Ratio Measures of Performance and Expected Relationship for Cooperatives and Investor-Owned Firms

Performance criteria	Ratio	Definition	Expected relationship
Profitability	Rate of return to equity (ROE)	Profit before tax* / Total equity	Coop < IOF
Leverage	Debt to equity	Total liabilities / Total equity	Coop > IOF
Solvency	Coverage ratio	Operating profit** / Interest expense	Coop < IOF
Liquidity	Quick ratio	Liquid Current Assets# / Current liabilities	Coop < IOF
Efficiency	Fixed asset turnover	Sales / Fixed assets	Coop < IOF
	Total asset turnover	Sales / Total assets	Coop < IOF
	Inventory turnover	Cost of Goods Sold / Inventory	Coop < IOF

* The before-tax rate of return on equity is used because some cooperatives do not report taxes in their income statement due to the possible impact of patronage refund policies on tax obligation. Also the available database for comparable IOFs reports only before-tax profit.
** Earnings before interest and tax (EBIT).
# Current assets less inventories.

25

2.3. Alternative Performance Criteria for Cooperatives

Cooperatives and IOFs are generally viewed as different in a number of nonfinancial dimensions and performance evaluation of cooperatives should not be limited to financial comparisons with IOFs. Cooperatives, in particular, are often thought of as providing a public good. One of the roles that cooperatives play, as suggested by Nourse (1922), is that of competitive yardstick: cooperatives should add enough competition to the system to give farmers a basis upon which to judge the terms offered by investor-owned firms. Staatz (1987, p. 97) notes that:

> Farmers, faced with unsatisfactory performance by IOFs, may form a cooperative firm whose purpose is to force the IOFs, through competition, to improve their service to farmers. If successful in enforcing competition, the cooperative generates benefits that it does not capture itself but which accrue to the farmer-stockholders, as well as to other farmers in the area.

Other public good aspects of cooperatives include their ability to correct for market failures by providing services for which a functioning market does not exist and their commitment to participatory management and democratic governance. Specific examples of the nonmarket services provided by dairy cooperatives in this study include the following: providing educational programs for farmer members in areas of management and production, offering a form of insurance through milk loss coverage for farm disasters, improving quality control standards at the farm level, promoting consumption of milk and dairy products through programs on nutrition, and interfacing between the farmer members and state cooperative associations.

Full evaluation of cooperative performance requires methods capable of valuing these nonmarket dimensions. Evaluation of nonmarket goods has received a great deal of consideration in the area of environmental and resource economics, where the two general approaches of evaluating nonmarket goods are: (1) inferring values from observed behavior, and (2) survey-based direct elicitation. Both approaches lend themselves to the evaluation of nonmarket aspects of cooperative performance.

With cooperatives viewed as a form of collective action, cooperative performance can be measured by estimating the incremental value of the cooperative to the members. An appropriate performance measure for an agricultural cooperative could be the profitability of the members' farming operations with and without the cooperative. For example, in the framework of approach (1) above, the incremental value of a marketing cooperative can be inferred from the differences in the prices received by member producers from their cooperative and those received by producers dealing with comparable IOFs. This approach is conceptually similar to hedonic pricing, a technique to value attributes for which no markets exist (see Nelson (1979) and Brookshire et al. (1982) for the evaluation of air pollution and airport noise).

Previous studies have looked at differences in prices between cooperatives and IOFs. Babb (1982) determined that dairy cooperatives paid higher prices for milk than IOFs. Additional Purdue University surveys looked at pricing differences between cooperatives and IOFs in other industries (Schrader et al. 1985). Although the differences observed were not always significant, the cooperatives on average appeared to price inputs lower and commodities higher than IOFs. These findings, however, were not used to measure the incremental value of cooperatives to their members.

Members and officers may also be interested in the valuation of specific cooperative attributes, such as training in democratic control or involvement in community development. This can be achieved by the survey-based direct elicitation methods, suggested in approach (2) above, which include contingent valuation, contingent ranking, and factorial survey methods (Cummings et al. 1986; Mitchell and Carson 1989; Smith and Desvouges 1986; Goodman 1989). Application of these techniques to empirical evaluation of cooperatives is a subject for future research.

In order to evaluate performance on cooperative-specific objectives which are not captured by financial ratio analysis, it is necessary to analyze nonmarket aspects of cooperative behavior. Boynton and Babb (1982) examined some nonfinancial aspects of cooperative performance, but they reported qualitative information, such as whether or not farmers perceived cooperatives as providing better service than IOFs, rather than an estimate of the incremental value of cooperatives to farmers. The techniques suggested above, such as hedonic pricing and contingent valuation, can be used for quantitative evaluation of nonmarket attributes of cooperatives. The expanded evaluation framework should improve our understanding of the performance of cooperatives and provide decision and policy makers with new tools for assessing cooperative behavior.

3. Methodology and Data

Financial economists generally agree that investor-owned firms may be viewed as value-maximizers and their performance can be measured by profitability adjusted for risk (Brealey and Myers 1991; Copeland and Weston 1983). The objective function of cooperatives is much less clearly defined, however, especially because the cooperative exists in order to provide a service to its members and the benefits of the cooperative form of organization are not restricted to earning a return on investment. As a result, there is a lack of accepted measures of cooperative performance.

The present research partially overcomes this difficulty by adopting a multidimensional approach. Four main measures of business performance are examined in different contexts: leverage, efficiency, liquidity, and profitability. Performance is analyzed by financial ratios based on reported accounting data, a standard technique borrowed from investor-owned firms for financial performance evaluation of cooperatives (Babb and Lang 1985; Chen, Babb, and Schrader 1985; Schrader et al. 1985). These performance measures focus on the cooperative as a business firm and do not capture possible additional benefits to members. Financial ratios reflect the effect of corporate strategic decisions (Brealey and Myers 1991) and should reveal if differences exist among cooperatives in different industries or in different countries, and also between cooperatives and investor-owned firms.

The performance measures in this research are analyzed over time, and not as point values. The dynamics of financial ratios provides valuable information about trends and changes over time, linking observed results to strategic decisions. The time-series accounting data are used to calculate the median of each financial ratio over the relevant sample of cooperatives for each observation year. The median was chosen as the descriptive statistic because it is more robust to outliers and gross errors in the data than the mean, an important advantage in small-sample analysis. The variability around the median in each year is estimated by the interquartile range. Differences between categories (size and industry, cooperatives and investor-owned firms, etc.) are tested for statistical significance by the nonparametric Wilcoxon test or Kruskal-Wallis test ("one-way analysis of variance by ranks") applied to samples of medians (Daniel 1990).

In the interest of comparability between U.S. and Israel, the research sample is based on regional service, marketing, and processing cooperatives in the two countries. The data base consists of a time series of annual financial reports of regional agricultural cooperatives in U.S. and Israel, covering a period of nearly 20 years from around 1970 to late 1980s.

The U.S. data were collected by writing to all the non-bargaining cooperatives listed in the ACS Directory of Farmer Cooperatives (Jermolowicz and Kennedy 1989). The sample includes 73 respondents that provided their annual reports in time for this research (the overall response rate to the mailing was over 20 percent). These are regional cooperatives with 1987 average sales of around $400 million which is similar in to the sales volume of the top 100 U.S. cooperatives regularly surveyed by the Agricultural Cooperative Service (Kane 1988).

The Israeli data were collected by personally meeting with the managers of regional enterprises in the kibbutz sector in order to persuade them to take part in the research. The annual financial statements of five regional conglomerates, representing over 35 individual enterprises, were obtained in time for inclusion in this research. This sample includes over 60 percent of the regional enterprises in Israel (five out of eight large-scale regional conglomerates). Given the secretive attitude toward accounting and financial data of privately held corporations in Israel in general and in the kibbutz sector in particular, this can be viewed as a very good achievement.

The financial data for investor-owned firms in the U.S. were obtained from Robert Morris Associates Annual Statement Studies (1971-1988), which regularly report a selection of median financial ratios for a wide range of industries, without interquartile ranges. In Israel, the performance measures of investor-owned firms in the relevant industries were calculated from the data published regularly by the Tel-Aviv Stock Exchange. The data for IOFs in Israel are restricted to publicly traded corporations, while the RMA data in the U.S. are based on a large sample of corporations, not all of which are publicly traded. Some of the U.S. fruit and vegetable processing cooperatives included in the sample operate on a pooling basis and do not include the cost of members' raw products in their income statement. For these cooperatives, cost of goods sold and profit before tax needed for efficiency and profitability measures (see Table 2.1) were estimated using an original adjustment technique developed in the process of this research (see Appendix).

4. Size and Industry Effects in the Performance of Agricultural Cooperatives

Performance evaluation of cooperatives has always been a topic of considerable interest in agricultural economics, primarily because of the significance of the cooperative form of organization in agriculture in both developed and developing countries. Traditionally, agricultural cooperatives have been encouraged as a vehicle for economic development, because the cooperative form of organization, in addition to being equitable, enables small producers to capture economies of size and increases their marketing power. Governments in both developed and developing countries actively promote and assist agricultural cooperatives. Justification of continued public support of the cooperative form of organization requires evaluation and monitoring of cooperative performance.

This chapter attempts to detect significant size and industry effects on performance among cooperatives. Size effects, if detected, may help to determine whether cooperatives should emphasize growth, as has been evident in the persistence of mergers among U.S. cooperatives. Industry effects, if found, may indicate whether the cooperative form of organization is more successful in the traditional industries of input supply and raw produce marketing than in the vertically integrated industries that include valued-added processing. The industry results may provide some evidence to resolve the conflict between cooperative strategists emphasizing traditional service activities and those advocating a shift toward value-added processing.

4.1. Data and Methodology

The research sample consisted of 43 US regional cooperatives for the period 1970-1987. The 43 regional cooperatives were classified into four industries: 12 dairy cooperatives, 12 supply cooperatives, 14 food marketing and processing cooperatives, and 5 grain and cotton marketing cooperatives.[2] The cooperatives were also classified into two size categories, "small" and "large," by their total assets. The range of mean total assets of the cooperatives in the sample was from $3 million to $911 million (averaged over the sample period). The distribution of mean asset size for the cooperatives is shown in Figure 4.1. For purposes of size analysis, 29 cooperatives with mean total assets of up to $125 million were classified as "small" and 14 cooperatives with mean total assets of over $125 million were classified as "large." The size classification threshold was identified by an agglomerative cluster analysis of the cooperatives by mean asset size. Figure 4.2 presents the distribution of the 43 cooperatives by industry and by size within each industry.

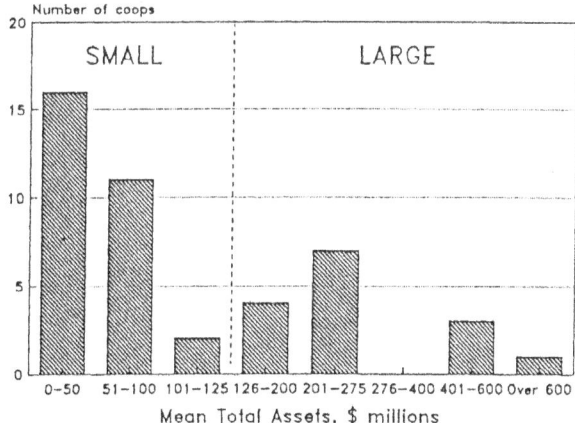

Figure 4.1. Distribution of mean assets.

---

[2] There was initial uncertainty as to the proper classification of grain and cotton cooperatives in the sample. Because grain marketing cooperatives also sell farm inputs to their members, it could be argued that they should be classified as supply cooperatives. Because cotton cooperatives operate on a pooling basis, it could be argued that they should be classified with the pooling food cooperatives. The uncertainty was resolved by applying multivariate discriminant analysis, which indicated that grain marketing cooperatives were distinct from the supply cooperatives and furthermore could be combined with the cotton cooperatives into one category. Discriminant analysis also established that cotton cooperatives could not be classified with food cooperatives. It was thus decided to classify the grain and cotton marketing cooperatives as a separate, although admittedly small, category.

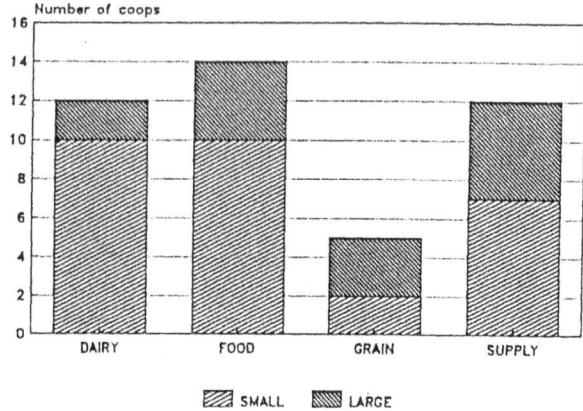

Figure 4.2. Distribution of cooperatives by industry and size:

SIZE	INDUSTRY				
	Dairy	Food	Grain	Supply	Total
Small	10	10	2	7	29
	(23%)	(23%)	(5%)	(16%)	(67%)
Large	2	4	3	5	14
	(5%)	(9%)	(7%)	(12%)	(33%)
Total	12	14	5	12	43
	(28%)	(32%)	(12%)	(28%)	(100%)

Table 4.1 presents the definitions of the subset of four financial ratios used in this analysis. These particular financial ratios were chosen because of their direct link to corporate strategy and objectives and their relevance for measuring the performance of cooperatives is discussed in Chapter 2.

TABLE 4.1: Financial Ratio Measures of Performance Used in this Study

Performance criteria	Ratio	Definition	Expected relationship
Leverage	Debt to equity	Total liabilities / Total equity	Coop > IOF
Efficiency	Fixed asset turnover	Sales / Fixed assets	Coop < IOF
Liquidity	Quick ratio	Liquid Current Assets# / Current liabilities	Coop < IOF
Profitability	Rate of return to equity (ROE)	Profit before tax* / Total equity	Coop < IOF

#, * See notes to Table 2.1.

The financial ratios of all the cooperatives were calculated from their audited annual reports for each year during the period 1970-1987. The time-series data were used to trace the behavior of cooperatives in different categories over time. For each observation year, the median of each of the four financial ratios was calculated separately in each industry and size category. In this way, a time series of 18 median observations was obtained for each financial ratio by industry and size categories.

The 1970-1987 time series of the median financial ratios were analyzed using the nonparametric Kruskal-Wallis test ("one-way analysis of variance by ranks") in order to detect significant differences among industry and size categories (Daniel 1990). In application to the two size categories, the Kruskal-Wallis test coincides with the Wilcoxon rank-sum test. The test ranks the pooled median financial ratios in different categories and forms the sums of the ranks for the pooled sample. If the rank sums, or the average scores, are sufficiently different among the categories, the test rejects the null hypothesis that the median financial ratios are the same across categories and establishes that, with a certain probability, the industry or size categories have different median financial ratios. The average rank scores in each category can be used to rank performance. The performance ranking of the different categories over the 1970-1987 period obtained in this was verified by Page's nonparametric test for ordered alternatives (Daniel 1990). Since the Page test results confirm and reinforce the Kruskal-Wallis test results, only the latter are reported in full.

In addition to tests of the performance ranking of categories, linear regression analysis of the median time series was used to identify differences in financial ratio trends by size and industry and to predict possible future changes in the performance rankings observed for the period 1970-1987. Trends were determined by running ordinary least-squares regressions for each median ratio on time with dummy variables for size and industry. The large cooperatives were the base for estimation of regression coefficients with size dummy variables, and the dairy category was the base for regression coefficient estimation with industry dummy variables. Two groups of tests were performed on the estimated regression coefficients: (a) homogeneity-of-slopes tests for significant difference of the estimated parameters between the base category and other categories and (b) multivariate tests for significant difference from zero of the sums of the estimated parameters corresponding to different size and industry categories.

4.2. Size Effects

Pronounced size effects were observed between large and small cooperatives over the period 1970-1987. The Kruskal-Wallis test results presented in Table 4.2 show that three of the four ratios (profitability, liquidity, and efficiency) were significantly different between the large and small cooperatives at the 0.05 level of significance. The median efficiency of asset utilization was significantly higher for the large cooperatives, while the median liquidity and profitability measures were significantly higher for the small cooperatives. Only the median leverage was not found to be significantly different between the two size categories.

TABLE 4.2: Test of Median Financial Ratios of Cooperatives by Size

| Ratio | Mean score | | Chi-Sq statistic | Prob > Chi-Sq* |
	Small	Large		
Debt to equity	17.3	19.7	0.48	0.486
Sales to assets	12.2	24.8	12.78	0.000
Quick ratio	24.4	12.6	11.25	0.000
Return on equity	23.9	13.1	9.42	0.002

* The probability that the Z-statistic exceeds the observed value under the null hypothesis that the median financial ratios are equal for the two size categories.

To illustrate the dispersion of the ratio values in each year, the top and bottom (25 percent and 75 percent) quartiles of the financial ratios were calculated for each year for the large and the small cooperatives. The interquartile range traces a band around the median that contains 50 percent of the observed ratio values in the sample of cooperatives for each particular year (this band is not necessarily symmetric about the median). The interquartile range is a nonparametric measure of dispersion analogous to standard deviation. Examination of the interquartile range of the two size categories over time provides a visual confirmation of the Kruskal-Wallis test results presented in Table 4.2.

Figure 4.3 (panels a to d) superimposes the interquartile range of small and large cooperatives for each ratio. Panel a shows that the interquartile range of the leverage ratio for the large cooperatives lies almost entirely within the interquartile range for the small cooperatives over the period 1970-1987. The overlapping interquartile ranges indicate that the median leverage is not significantly different for the small and the large cooperatives.

In panel b, the interquartile range of the efficiency ratio for the large cooperatives lies within the interquartile range for the small cooperatives until about 1979, after which the top quartile value of the large cooperatives is consistently higher than the top quartile value of the small cooperatives. The graphical presentation reveals that the difference between large and small cooperatives became more pronounced over the later period 1979-1987. Large cooperatives thus appear to be more efficient than the small cooperatives in utilizing their assets to generate sales.

In panel c, the top quartile of the liquidity ratio for the small cooperatives consistently lies above the top quartile for the large cooperatives, while the bottom quartiles roughly overlap. This indicates that the small cooperatives maintain a higher liquidity than the large ones.

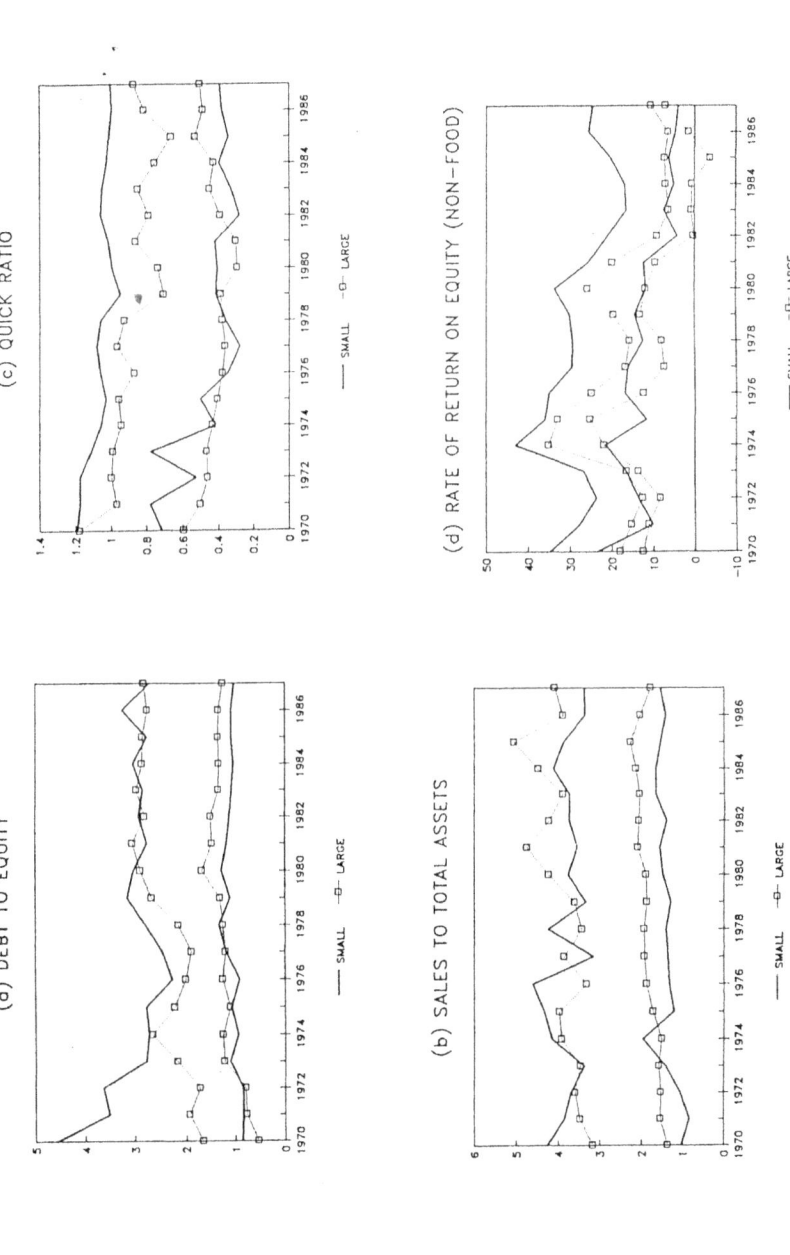

Figure 4.3. Interquartile range of the financial ratios by size category, 1970-1987.

Panel d presents the interquartile range of the profitability ratio. The upper quartile of the rate of return on equity (ROE) for the small cooperatives lies above the upper ROE quartile for the large cooperatives in 17 out of 18 years, and the bottom quartile of the small cooperatives lies above the bottom quartile of the large cooperatives in 14 out of the 18 years. The ROE for the small cooperatives is thus observed to be higher over most of the sample period than for the large cooperatives.

Trend analysis results for the median financial ratios of the large and the small cooperatives are presented in Table 4.3. The median leverage ratio shows significantly different trends for the two size categories, increasing over time for the large cooperatives and declining for the small cooperatives. If this difference continues, large cooperatives may develop in the future significantly higher levels of debt relative to equity than the small cooperatives, contrary to the pattern observed between 1970 and 1987 (Figure 4.3a). The median efficiency of the large cooperatives increases over time, while that of the small cooperatives declines, which should only strengthen in the future the advantage that large cooperatives had between 1970 and 1987 in utilizing their assets to generate sales (Figure 4.3b). Both profitability and liquidity reveal a declining trend, but the rate of decline is not significantly different for the large and the small cooperatives, which suggests that the advantage in profitability and liquidity observed for the small cooperatives between 1970 and 1987 may be maintained in the future.

TABLE 4.3: Estimated Trend of Median Financial Ratios by Size, 1970-1987

Ratio	Large	Small	Adj. R-square
Debt to equity	0.03[a]	−0.04[a,b]	0.34
Sales to assets	0.03[a]	−0.03[a,b]	0.46
Quick ratio	−0.01[a]	−0.02[a,c]	0.68
Return on equity	−0.74[a]	−0.72[a,c]	0.54

[a] Indicates significantly different from 0 at 0.05 level.

[b] Indicates significantly different from Large at 0.05 level.

[c] Indicates not significantly different from Large at 0.05 level.

Thus, while the large cooperatives are observed to be more efficient in utilizing their assets to generate sales, the small cooperatives have higher profitability and liquidity. The results suggest that large cooperatives may enjoy scale economies in terms of efficiency, but the benefits of size do not necessarily translate into higher profitability. The higher rate of return on equity for the small cooperatives is consistent with the "small-firm effect" observed for investor-owned corporations, which shows that investors in small firms usually earn higher rates of return on investment (see Levy and Lerman (1985) and references therein). With respect to liquidity, it could be hypothesized that small firms, with a relatively small asset base, prefer to maintain a higher liquidity buffer than large, asset-rich firms. With respect to leverage, it could similarly be argued that small cooperatives would have a lower leverage than the large, more secure cooperatives. While the results for the period 1970-1987 fail to detect significant differences in capital structure between small and large cooperatives, the trend analysis results support an expectation of higher leverage for the large cooperatives.

4.3. Industry Effects

Clear industry effects were found for all median financial ratios. The Kruskal-Wallis test results (Table 4.4) show that for leverage, efficiency, and liquidity the industry effects were significant at 0.01 level. The statistical test results are visually confirmed by the time series graphs in Figure 4.4 (panels a to d). The graphs in Figure 4.4 plot only the median ratios by industry over the period 1970-1987, as it was not practicable to superimpose the interquartile ranges for the four industries.

TABLE 4.4: Kruskal-Wallis Rank Test of Median Financial Ratios of Cooperatives

Ratio	Mean score				Chi-Sq statistic	Prob > Chi-Sq*
	Dairy	Food	Grain	Supply		
Debt to equity	34.8	57.1	44.1	10.0	48.8	0.000
Sales to assets	60.4	9.5	48.4	27.7	28.5	0.000
Quick ratio	59.2	21.6	15.8	49.4	54.6	0.000
Return on equity	39.7	35.9	42.9	27.5	5.4	0.143

* The probability that the Chi-Sq statistic (the large-sample approximation of the Kruskal-Wallis statistic) exceeds the observed value under the null hypothesis that the median financial ratios are equal for the four industry groups.

The leverage ratio (panel a) was found to be the highest for the food marketing cooperatives and the lowest for the supply cooperatives, with the dairy and grain cooperatives lying in the middle.

The four industries are also clearly differentiated by efficiency (panel b). Dairies consistently have the highest efficiency, followed by grain and supply cooperatives in this order, with the food marketing cooperatives consistently at the bottom of the ranking.

Liquidity is the highest for dairy and supply cooperatives, which both have relatively high quick ratios near the level of 1.0 (panel c), while food and grain cooperatives have relatively low quick ratios around 0.5. The Kruskal-Wallis test indicates that only the differences between the food and grain cooperatives are not significant.

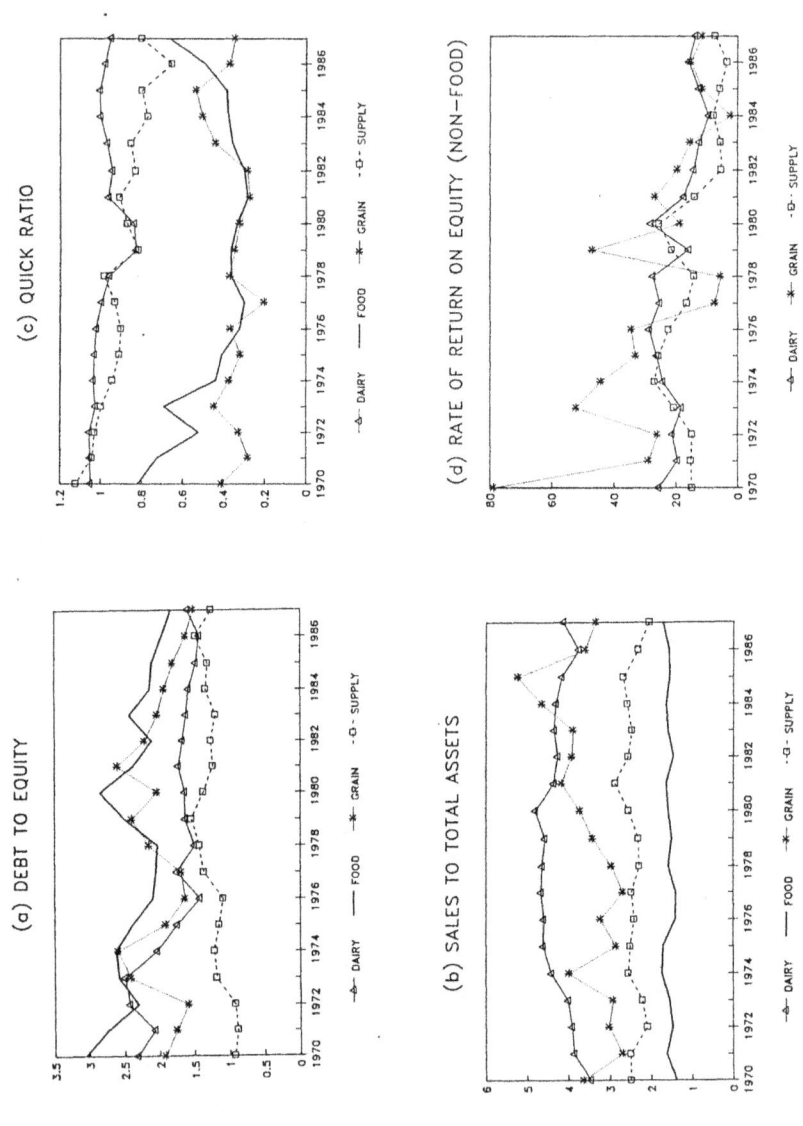

Figure 4.4. Median financial ratios by industry, 1970-1987.

The differences in profitability between dairy, food, and grain cooperatives are not statistically significant. Yet the median ROE of the cooperatives in these three industries combined is significantly higher than that of the supply cooperatives (at 0.05 level of significance by the Kruskal-Wallis test).

TABLE 4.5: Estimated Trend of Median Financial Ratios by Industry, 1970-1987

Ratio	Dairy	Food	Grain	Supply	Adj. R-square
Debt to equity	-0.05^a	$-0.04^{a,c}$	-0.01^b	$0.02^{a,b}$	0.74
Sales to assets	0.01	0.01^c	$0.07^{a,b}$	0.00^c	0.89
Quick ratio	-0.01	$-0.01^{a,c}$	0.00^c	$-0.02^{a,b}$	0.90
Return on equity	-0.74^a	-0.31^c	$-1.79^{a,b}$	$-0.93^{a,c}$	0.34

a Indicates significantly different from 0 at 0.05 level.
b Indicates significantly different from Dairy at 0.05 level.
c Indicates not significantly different from Dairy at 0.05 level.

The trends of the median financial ratios by industry are presented in Table 4.5. The median debt to equity ratios of the cooperatives in the four industries show a converging trend, mainly as a result of the declining leverage of the dairy and food cooperatives and the increasing leverage of the supply cooperatives (compare Figure 4.4a). It might be conjectured that the highly leveraged food and dairy cooperatives benefited from erosion of their fixed-rate debt in the inflationary period 1973-1980: their equity component may have increased through unrealized capital gains, driving the leverage ratio down over time. The median sales to assets ratio of the dairy, food, and supply cooperatives does not show a significant trend over time, and the relative efficiency ranking of these industries will probably be maintained in the future (Figure 4.4b). The grain cooperatives show a significant improvement of their sales to assets ratio, and as a result may challenge in the future the top ranking dairy cooperatives. The rate of return on equity (ROE) reveals a significant declining trend for cooperatives in three of the four industries; only the estimated coefficient of the food cooperatives, while negative, is not significantly different from zero. The estimated decline in median ROE may be due to the general downturn in the US agricultural sector during the 1980s, as separate analysis using only the 1970-1979 data did not reveal significant downward trends in profitability during the pre-1980 decade for three out of the four industries (except the grain cooperatives).

In summary, on a naive multiobjective scale that assigns equal weights to the four ratios (Table 4.6), the dairy cooperatives appear to be the strongest performers among the four industries, ranking first in efficiency and liquidity and second in leverage and profitability. The food marketing cooperatives are the weakest performers, ranking lowest in leverage, efficiency, and liquidity. The supply and grain cooperatives are in the middle of the ranking.

TABLE 4.6: Multiobjective Performance Scores of Cooperatives by Industry, 1970-1987 (1 = Lowest, 4 = Highest)

	Profitability	Leverage*	Efficiency	Liquidity	Unweighted score
Dairy	3	3	4	4	3.50
Food	3	1	1	1.5	1.63
Grain	3	2	3	1.5	2.38
Supply	1	4	2	3	2.50

* Leverage scores are assigned in the reverse order of the numerical values of the leverage ratio, because low leverage is considered superior to high leverage due to the lower associated risk.

4.4. Conclusion

One of the persistent trends among cooperatives is growth through mergers and acquisitions. The findings of this study indicate that although larger cooperatives improve efficiency through economies of scale, the higher efficiency of asset utilization does not translate into higher profitability. This suggests that the benefits of mergers may be over-emphasized, which is consistent with recent findings indicating that the profitability of cooperatives does not significantly improve after a merger (Parliament and Taitt 1989).

The industry effects revealed in this study do not provide conclusive evidence to support either side of the strategic conflict between the advocates of traditional service activities and the advocates of diversification through value-added processing. The dairy cooperatives, which engage in value-added processing, are the highest ranking performers among the four industries by leverage, efficiency, liquidity, and profitability ratios. The food cooperatives, on the other hand, are at the bottom of the ranking, although they also engage in extensive value-added processing.

The grain and supply cooperatives, which have generally limited their activities to the traditional areas of raw produce marketing and input purchasing, show a higher performance ranking than the food cooperatives engaging in value-added processing. It could be argued that the relatively strong performance of the dairy cooperatives in the US is related to government guaranteed prices for the milk used in dairy products. If this is indeed so, the inferior performance of the food processing cooperatives may be interpreted as consistent with the view that, in the absence of specific support programs for value-added processing, cooperatives should consider restricting their scope to traditional activities.

In the comparison of cooperatives and investor-owned firms (see Chapter 5), the food cooperatives were found to have a weaker performance than the investor-owned firms in the same industry by three of the six performance measures considered while the dairy cooperatives performed not worse than the investor-owned dairies by all measures. These findings indicate that the relatively weak performance of the food cooperatives observed in the present study cannot be entirely attributed to industry-specific factors. There are indications that, of the two value-added processing industries, the dairy cooperatives have a higher proportion of pass-through sales than the food-processing cooperatives: the proportion of fluid milk sales in dairies is higher than the proportion of raw produce sales in food-processing cooperatives. These factors also could be interpreted as supporting the view that expansion into value-added processing has not been a total success for cooperatives.

An international comparison is provided by a study of two regional agricultural cooperatives in Israel (Yacobi 1989), where the cooperative engaging in value-added food processing had significantly higher leverage, lower profitability, and lower efficiency than the cooperative that limited its activities to raw produce marketing. The Israeli analogy, however limited, appears to support those who believe that manufacturing of value-added consumer products may not be a particularly advantageous activity for cooperatives, despite the allure of forward integration. Cooperatives may find it difficult to acquire the necessary resources for successful penetration of the consumer food markets.

Support programs, product mix, and market characteristics are ultimately responsible for success or failure of value-added processing. Further research is needed in order to identify and separate the government support component in the performance of U.S. dairy cooperatives and to analyze the cooperatives in the two valued-added processing industries on the basis of the specific mix of pass-through sales and value-added products. More detailed comparisons between cooperatives and investor-owned firms in corresponding industries are needed in order to separate between industry-specific and cooperative-specific factors. This additional research may produce more conclusive results regarding the debate between supporters of traditional cooperatives and advocates of vertical integration. At this stage, the striking difference in performance between the two valued-added processing industries in our sample makes it difficult to generalize about the relative merits of value-added processing for cooperatives.

5. Comparative Performance of U.S. Cooperatives and Investor-Owned Firms

The underlying hypothesis of this research is that cooperative-specific factors, which include moral hazard behavior, nonmarketability of equity, and horizon problems, are theoretically expected to produce inferior performance of cooperatives relative to investor-owned forms (IOFs) as measured by standard financial criteria. Yet cooperatives operate in the same competitive environment as IOFs and are exposed to the same market forces. It is therefore relevant to examine whether the difference in objectives between cooperatives and investor-owned firms outweighs the effect of the similarities in business functions. This question is examined through comparative analysis of financial performance of cooperatives and investor-owned firms in two food industries in the U.S. agribusiness sector – fruit and vegetable processors and dairy product manufacturers. Agribusinesses are chosen as the research base because of the prominence of cooperatives in agriculture. In the last decades, nearly 30 percent of all farm products and 20 percent of all farm inputs in the US were handled by cooperatives, and in some states the cooperative share is as high as 50 percent (Biser and O'Day 1984).

5.1. Data and Methodology

The data for the comparative analysis of U.S. cooperatives and IOFs included a sample of 18 regional cooperatives: 9 cooperatives specializing in canned and frozen fruits, vegetables, and juices and 9 dairy cooperatives processing fluid milk and manufacturing value-added dairy products, such as butter, cheese, ice cream, and yogurt. Fruit and vegetable cooperatives that are mainly wholesalers of fresh produce and dairies that mainly sell fluid milk were excluded from the sample.

The performance of cooperatives and IOFs was evaluated using six financial ratios (see Table 5.1):

(1)   rate of return to equity (before tax) as a measure profitability,

(2)   the ratio of debt to equity as a measure of capital structure and exposure to financial risk,

(3)   the ratio of operating earnings to interest (coverage ratio) as a measure of solvency,

(4+5) fixed asset turnover (the ratio of sales to fixed assets) and inventory turnover (the ratio of cost of goods to inventory) as measures of asset utilization efficiency,

(6)   the quick ratio (the ratio of liquid current assets to current liabilities) as a measure of liquidity.

The financial ratios of the cooperatives were calculated from their audited annual reports for the period 1976-1987. For each observation year, the median of each of the six financial ratios was calculated for each of the two cooperative industries. Two time series of 12 median observations were thus obtained for each ratio – one for the fruit and vegetable cooperatives and the other for the dairy cooperatives. Medians had to be used for cooperatives because the available source of IOF data included medians, and not means, as the descriptive statistics. The use of medians is actually an advantage for small samples, as in this research, because medians are more robust to outliers and gross errors in the data than the means.

The financial data for IOFs were obtained from Robert Morris Associates Annual Statement Studies (RMA), which report a selection of median financial ratios for a wide range of industries. IOFs with operations comparable to the dairy cooperatives were represented by the Dairy Product Manufacturers category (SIC nos. 2021-24, 2026), which does not include firms primarily engaged in sales of bulk milk. No single IOF category matched exactly the operations of the fruit and vegetable processing cooperatives, and therefore two industrial classifications were used: Manufacturers of Canned and Dried Fruits and Vegetables (SIC nos. 2033-34) and Manufacturers of Frozen Fruits, Fruit Juices, and Vegetables (SIC no. 2037). Over the years covered by the study, the number of manufacturers of dairy products included in the RMA database ranged from 89 to 160; the number of manufactures of canned and dried fruits and vegetables ranged from 69 to 98; and the number of manufacturers of frozen fruits, fruit juices and vegetables ranged from 18 to 31. In addition to being comparable with respect to the scope of operations, all the firms were of comparable size – between $10 million and $100 million in average total assets.

To detect significant differences between cooperatives and IOFs, the 1976-1987 time series of the median financial ratios in each industry were analyzed using the nonparametric Kruskal-Wallis test, also known as "one-way analysis of variance by ranks" (Daniel 1990). The test ranks the pooled median financial ratios in the different firm categories in each industry and forms the sums of the ranks for the pooled sample. If the rank sums, or the average scores, are sufficiently different between the IOF and cooperative categories, the test rejects the null hypothesis that the median financial ratios are the same for the two types of firms and establishes that, with a certain probability, the cooperatives and IOFs in a particular industry have different median financial ratios. Moreover, the average rank scores in each category can be used to determine if the performance measures of cooperatives are greater or less than those of IOFs.

5.2. Results of Financial Ratio Analysis

The 1976-1987 time series of the six median ratios for cooperatives and IOFs in the two industries are presented in Figure 5.1. The thick solid lines plot the cooperative ratios and the broken lines plot the IOF ratios. Separate time series are shown for the two IOF industrial classifications to which the fruit and vegetable cooperatives are compared.

Panels a-c in Figure 5.1 present the three ratios related to profitability and capital structure – the rate of return to equity, the debt to equity ratio, and the ratio of operating earnings to interest. In the fruit and vegetable processing industry, the three ratios for the IOFs overlap the corresponding ratios for the comparable cooperatives. The Kruskal-Wallis test indicates that these three median ratios are not significantly different for the cooperatives and IOFs in the fruit and vegetable industry. In the dairy industry, the rate of return to equity (panel a) is also not significantly different between IOFs and cooperatives, but both the debt to equity ratio (panel b) and the earnings to interest ratio (panel c) are significantly different. By both ratios, the dairy cooperatives outperform the dairy IOFs – the debt to equity ratio is lower and the earnings to interest ratio is higher.

The three median ratios related to current operations (panels d-f in Figure 5.1) reveal significant differences in cooperative and IOF performance in both industries. The differences, however, are in opposite directions.

The ratio of sales to fixed assets (panel d) indicates that fruit and vegetable cooperatives were consistently less efficient in utilizing their fixed assets to generate sales than IOFs, whereas the dairy cooperatives were more efficient than the comparable IOFs.

Fruit & Vegetable   Dairy

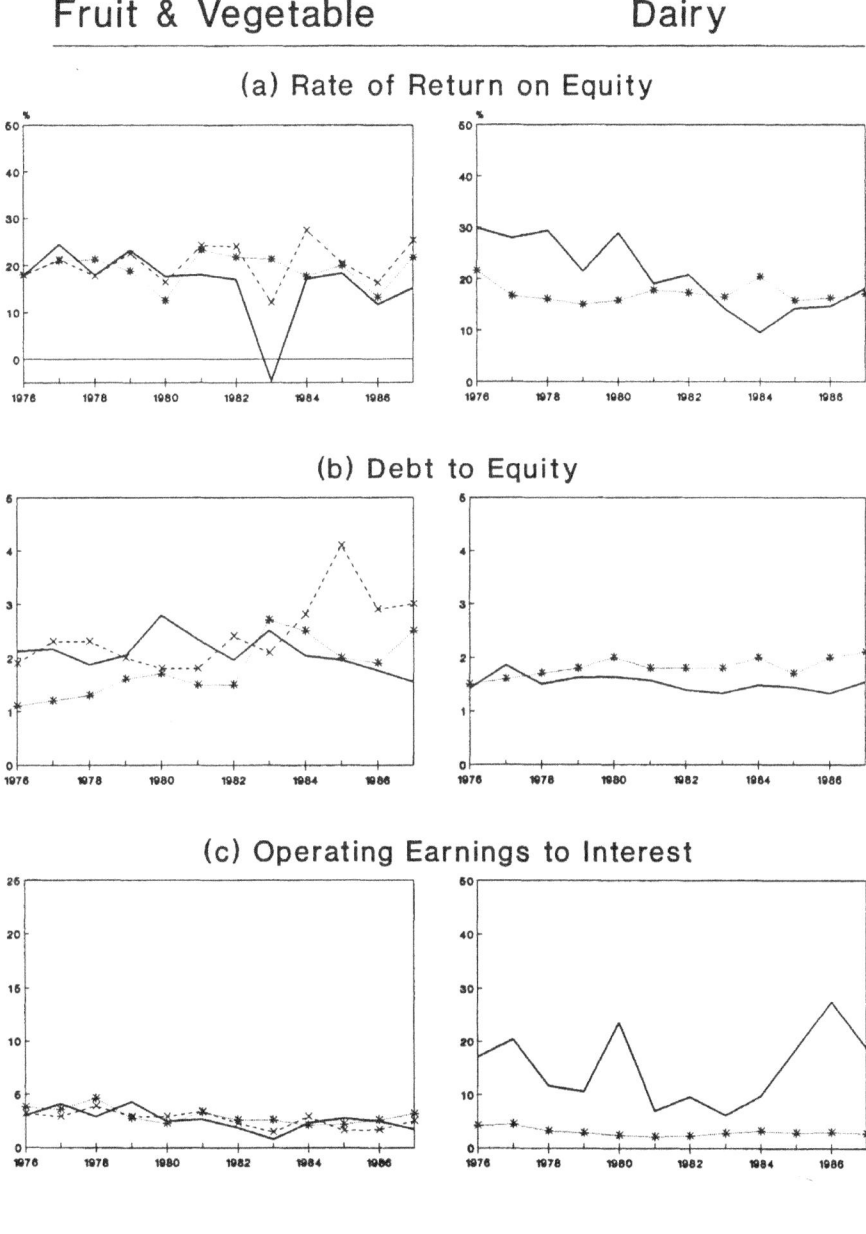

(a) Rate of Return on Equity

(b) Debt to Equity

(c) Operating Earnings to Interest

- ··×·· IOFS: FROZEN   ─*─ IOFS: CANNED & DAIRY   ─── COOPS

Figure 5.1. Median financial ratios for cooperatives and IOFs in the fruit and vegetable and dairy industries.

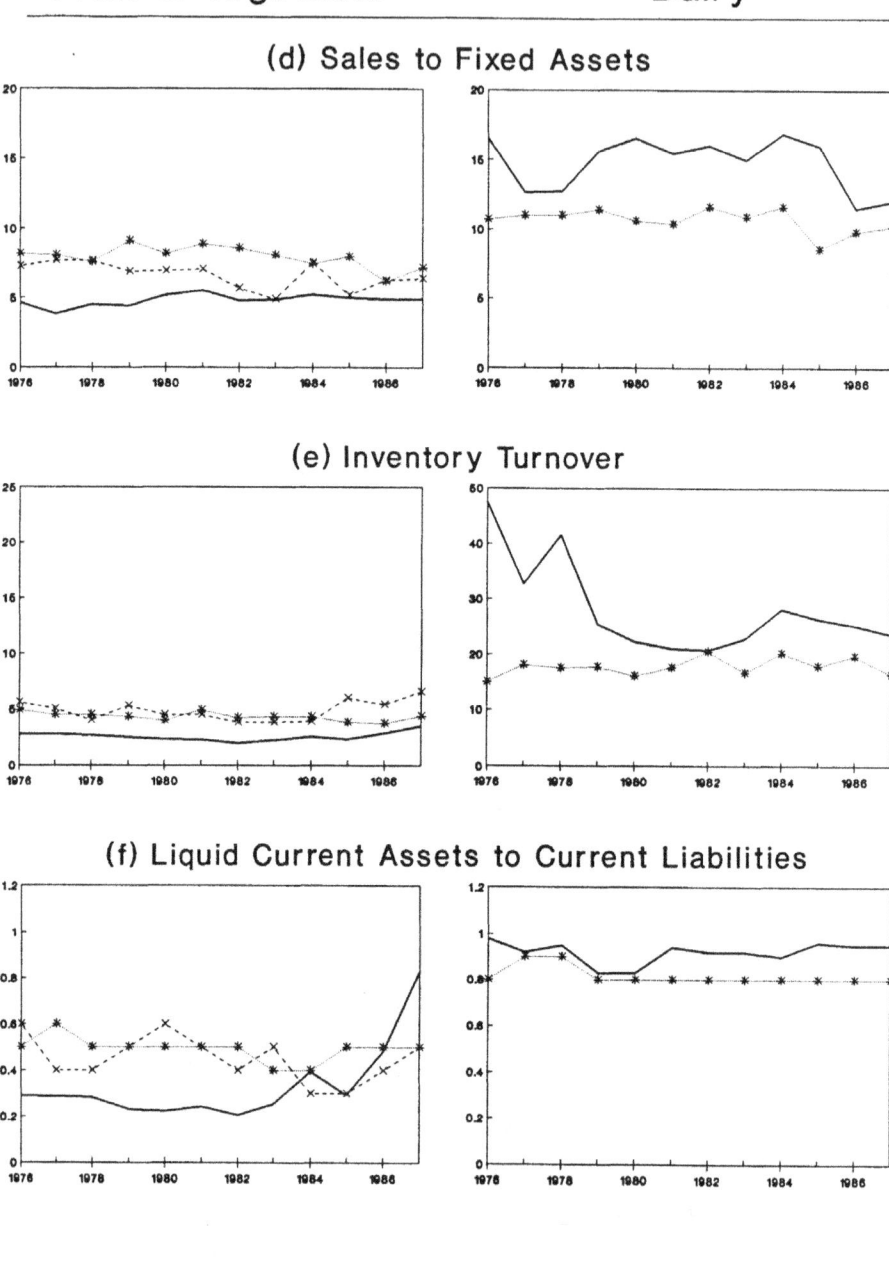

Fruit & Vegetable   Dairy

(d) Sales to Fixed Assets

(e) Inventory Turnover

(f) Liquid Current Assets to Current Liabilities

··×·· IOFS: FROZEN   ─*─ IOFS: CANNED & DAIRY   ── COOPS

Figure 5.1 (continued).

46

The inventory turnover (panel e) indicates that fruit and vegetable cooperatives were carrying higher levels of inventories relative to sales than the comparable IOFs, whereas the dairy cooperatives were carrying lower inventory levels relative to sales than the dairy IOFs.

The quick ratio, defined as the ratio of liquid current assets to current liabilities (panel f), was consistently higher for dairy cooperatives than for comparable IOFs, whereas for fruit and vegetable cooperatives it was lower than for IOFs over most of the years. These quick ratio comparisons indicate that dairy cooperatives maintained a higher liquidity level, while the fruit and vegetable cooperatives maintained a lower liquidity level compared to IOFs in their industry.

Table 5.1 summarizes the comparative performance findings. Contrary to the relationships suggested by the initial hypotheses (see Table 2.1), cooperatives in both industries were not found to be inferior to comparable IOFs by the rate of return on equity, the debt to equity ratio, and the ratio of earnings to interest. In contrast, the three current operations measures observed for the fruit and vegetable cooperatives were consistent with the hypotheses that suggest lower performance for cooperatives than for comparable IOFs. The dairy cooperatives, on the other hand, performed significantly better than the dairy IOFs by the three current operations measures.

TABLE 5.1: Comparison of cooperatives and IOFs in the fruit and vegetable and the dairy industries

Ratio	Fruit & Vegetables	Dairy
Profitability and Capital Structure		
Rate of Return to Equity	Coops ≈ IOFs	Coops ≈ IOFs
Debt to Equity	Coops ≈ IOFs	Coops ≈ IOFs
Operating Earnings to Interest	Coops ≈ IOFs	Coops > IOFs*
Current Operations		
Sales to Fixed Assets	Coops < IOFs*	Coops > IOFs*
Inventory Turnover	Coops < IOFs*	Coops > IOFs*
Liquid Current Assets to Current Liabilities	Coops < IOFs*	Coops > IOFs*

* The corresponding ratios are significantly different between cooperatives and IOFs at 0.05 significance level by the Kruskal-Wallis test.

The results indicate that the observed poorer performance of the fruit and vegetable cooperatives compared to cooperatives in other industries (see Chapter 4) cannot be attributed solely to industry-specific factors. An examination of the distinctive features of cooperatives and IOFs in each industry is required in order to account for these differences.

It could be argued that the higher sales to fixed assets ratio and inventory turnover for the dairy cooperatives is caused by a higher proportion of fluid milk sales for cooperatives than IOFs. Fluid milk sales do not require as high a level of fixed assets as value added processing and, being perishable, generate a higher turnover rate than processed products. Indeed, as the dairy cooperatives shifted into more value-added processing during the 1970s, the proportion of fluid milk sales declined and the inventory turnover decreased markedly (panel e). This trend, however, did not result in a corresponding decrease of the sales to fixed assets ratio (panel d). The advantage that dairy cooperatives exhibit relative to IOFs in generating sales from their fixed assets thus cannot be entirely attributed to fluid milk sales, and may be an indication of higher operating efficiency.

Fruit and vegetable processors, unlike dairies, deal with a variety of nonhomogeneous raw products subject to relative changes in consumer demand. While IOFs are free to choose their suppliers depending on changing demand patterns, cooperatives are committed to serving their members and as a result are often locked into an existing product mix, at least in the short run. Inflexibility in controlling the mix of the members' products may place the cooperatives at a disadvantage in this industry, and inadequate product mix may cause the cooperatives to miss market opportunities. Cooperatives may also suffer from adverse selection of members, and the resulting effect on quality may prevent them from getting top prices for their products. In either case, the fruit and vegetable cooperatives are unable to maximize sales for a given asset base, which is reflected in lower sales to fixed assets ratios and lower inventory turnovers compared to IOFs.

Differences in the quick ratio between cooperatives and IOFs were analyzed by examining the balance sheet composition. Cooperatives in both industries were found to carry a higher proportion of current liabilities than the comparable IOFs. For cooperatives, these current liabilities were primarily funds owed for members' products. Fruit and vegetable cooperatives, however, were observed to have a substantially lower proportion of accounts receivable than the comparable IOFs, which accounts for their lower quick ratio. The dairy cooperatives, in addition to the higher proportion of current liabilities, also carried a higher proportion of accounts receivable than the comparable IOFs. The relative increase in accounts receivable, however, was greater than the relative increase in current liabilities, which accounts for the higher quick ratio of the dairy cooperatives compared to IOFs.

The higher proportion of accounts receivable for the dairy cooperatives could result from relatively liberal credit terms to customers. The cooperatives apparently support this policy by delaying the payments to their members, as evidenced by their higher proportion of current liabilities.

This credit policy would enhance their sales, which is consistent with the higher sales to fixed assets ratio observed for the dairy cooperatives. For the fruit and vegetable cooperatives, on the other hand, the lower proportion of accounts receivable compared to the IOFs may reflect more stringent credit terms than those adopted by the rest of the industry. More restrictive credit terms may result in lower sales and thus account in part for the lower sales to fixed assets ratio of these cooperatives.

5.3. Fixed Asset Growth

The lower sales to fixed assets ratio of the fruit and vegetable cooperatives relative to the comparable IOFs may be interpreted as a symptom of "overinvestment". An alternative way to assess overinvestment tendencies is by examining growth, as firms investing in excess capacity are likely to have relatively high fixed asset growth rates.

TABLE 5.2: Mean Annual Growth Rates of Fixed Assets for Cooperatives and IOFs in the Fruit and the Dairy Industries Estimated from Semilogarithmic Regression (percent)

Product	Cooperatives	IOFs
Fruit & Vegetables[a]	7.5	9.6
Dairy	11.1[b]	9.6

[a] The two IOF industry classifications representing canned and dried fruits and vegetable and frozen fruits, vegetables, and juices were both included in the regression, because a preliminary analysis showed that their asset growth rates were not significantly different.

[b] Significantly different at the 0.05 level from the estimated growth rate for the fruit & vegetable cooperatives by the test for homogeneity of slopes in dummy variable regression. All other growth rates are not significantly different from one another at the 0.05 level.

Mean annual growth rates of fixed assets were estimated separately for cooperatives and IOFs in the two industries (Table 5.2). Because of the limitations imposed by the available fixed-asset data for IOFs, the growth rates were estimated for the "average" firm in each category: the "average" firm fixed assets were determined by dividing the sum of fixed assets of the sample firms by the number of firms. A semi-logarithmic regression was used to estimate the growth rates, assuming the standard compound growth model

$$FA_t = F_0(1 + g)^t$$

where FA_t stands for fixed assets in year t and g is the mean annual growth rate. The explanatory variables in the regression included dummies for organizational structure (cooperatives or IOFs) and industry effects (fruit and vegetable processors or dairies).

The test for homogeneity of slopes indicated that there were no significant differences between the fixed asset growth rates of cooperatives and IOFs in each industry. Within organizational categories, the dairy cooperatives had a significantly higher mean growth rate than the fruit and vegetable cooperatives, but there were no significant differences in the growth rate between IOFs in the two industries.

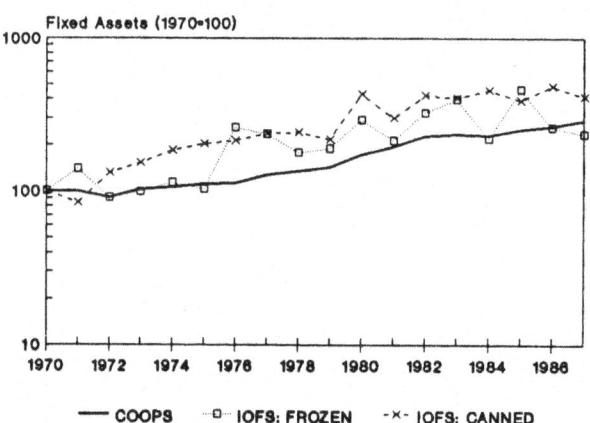

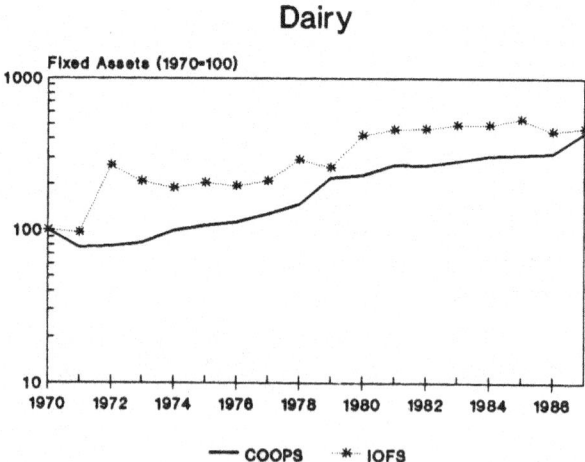

Figure 5.2. Growth of fixed assets of cooperatives and IOFs in the fruit and vegetable and dairy industries (1970=100).

Figure 5.2 plots the growth of average fixed assets over time for the dairy and the fruit and vegetable industries. The graphs visually confirm the estimated growth rates reported in Table 5.2: the growth rates are not dramatically different between cooperatives and IOFs in each industry. Therefore, the lower fixed asset utilization of the fruit and vegetable cooperatives is currently the only evidence of overinvestment by food-processing cooperatives.

The similarity of asset growth rates between cooperatives and IOFs is also relevant for the interpretation of the debt to equity findings (see Figure 5.1, panel b). Although cooperative borrowing levels are lower than initially hypothesized, cooperatives achieved the same growth rates as the comparable IOFs, without visible signs of capital starvation. Thus, lack of investment opportunities or externally imposed restrictions on borrowing cannot by cited to explain why the cooperative debt was found to be lower than expected. Perhaps, as suggested by Caves and Petersen (1986), differences in tax treatment between cooperatives and IOFs enlarge a cooperative's stream of internal finance per dollar of net margin, thus allowing a cooperative to achieve comparable growth rates with lower debt to equity ratios.

5.4. Concluding Comments

The performance comparisons between US cooperatives and IOFs in two food industries using standard financial ratio analysis do not provide strong evidence in support of the initial hypotheses which suggested that cooperatives could be expected to exhibit low profitability, relatively high borrowing, and overinvestment in fixed assets and inventories (see Table 2.1). The rate of return to equity in cooperatives was not found to be significantly different from that of IOFs in the comparable industries; the debt to equity and the earnings to interest ratios for cooperatives were not found to be higher than for the comparable IOFs; and no compelling evidence for overinvestment was found for cooperatives in either industry.

The observation that the reported profitability of cooperatives was better than expected and comparable to that of IOFs cannot be attributed to a low equity base in cooperatives. The proportion of equity in the cooperatives was not lower than that of the comparable IOFs. In fact, the dairy cooperatives were observed to have a significantly lower debt to equity ratio than the dairy IOFs, which indicates a relatively large equity base. These results counter the view that cooperatives are "equity bound."

The finding that cooperatives, while maintaining the same growth rates as IOFs, do not rely more heavily on debt financing and do not maintain lower safety margins against default is similarly inconsistent with the hypothesis of moral hazard behavior, which suggests that cooperatives may be willing to assume higher risks because of the "safety net" provided by the principles of mutual aid and responsibility.

On the overinvestment issue, the findings conclusively indicate that the dairy cooperatives are not overinvested: they utilize their fixed assets more efficiently in generating sales than the comparable IOFs, while maintaining comparable long-term growth rates. The conclusions are not as clear with regard to the fruit and vegetable cooperatives. Their relatively low sales to fixed assets ratio is a symptom of overinvestment. However, there has been a significant improvement in this ratio over time relative to the rest of the industry (see Figure 5.1, panel d). The findings suggest that the extent of overinvestment, although initially present, has diminished over time as cooperatives increased the utilization of their asset base to generate sales. The initial overinvestment may be a reflection of the indivisibility of new investments in fixed assets made in the early 1970s as the fruit and vegetable cooperatives moved into more value-added processing. The entry into new product lines may have involved unavoidable excess capacity, or "overinvestment," but the utilization of capacity improved as sales increased over time. The lack of clear evidence of overinvestment in the fruit and vegetable and the dairy cooperatives contrasts with the findings of Sexton (1989), who observed overinvestment for cotton ginning cooperatives. This may be another reflection of industry effects that have been previously observed to produce differences in various performance measures among cooperatives.

The relatively conservative capital structure and lack of overinvestment on the part of cooperatives do not support the hypothesis of cooperative susceptibility to moral hazard behavior. The immobility of cooperative equity and the members' largely undiversified investment in the agricultural sector may cause cooperative members to be more risk averse than IOF shareholders with their more liquid, diversified portfolios. As a result, pressure exerted by members may counteract in part the hypothesized tendency of cooperatives to accept higher risks.

Lang et al. (1985) report in their survey that policy makers and university economists felt that there were significant differences in goals between cooperatives and IOFs. On the other hand, managers of cooperatives and IOFs ranked their goals essentially the same. The findings of this paper suggest that the standards of financial analysis in the business community may have "forced" cooperatives to adopt virtually the same goals as investor-owned firms, in line with the views expressed by the surveyed practitioners. The emphasis on efficiency and return on investment in the financial community may have had a determining influence on the behavior of cooperatives.

The observed similarity in the reported profitability of cooperatives and IOFs indicates that the overall benefits received by members from their cooperative may exceed the benefits received by shareholders from IOFs in the form of return on equity. This implication requires further study using non-accounting techniques to value the supplementary benefits of membership in a cooperative (see Chapter 2, Sec. 2.3).

6. Financing of Growth in Agricultural Cooperatives

Increasing complexity and sophistication of markets and technology has stimulated a trend toward growth, conglomeration, and geographical expansion of investor-owned agribusinesses (van Dijk and Veerman 1990). There is evidence that higher market share achieved through growth is positively correlated with higher profitability (Buzzell and Wiersema 1981) – an objective pursued by both shareholders and managers in investor-owned firms.

Cooperatives also must grow if they are to maintain their competitive posture and to continue providing services to their members. In fact Schrader (1989b) found that management felt growth was essential for their cooperatives to remain viable, and Koller (1972-73) suggests that "cooperatives need to grow to take advantage of a continuum of new technologies, new opportunities for economies of size, and increased efficiency...". In line with this philosophy and spurred by competitive pressures from investor-owned agribusinesses, agricultural cooperatives in the U.S. have shown a high frequency of consolidations, increasing the average sales volume per cooperative. The number of farm supply and marketing cooperatives declined by more than one third over the decade 1976-1985, while the cooperatives' share of farm supply purchases increased from 18 percent to 26 percent and the share of farm products marketed remained near 28 percent (U.S. Department of Agriculture 1987).

Growth requires financing which, for investor-owned firms, can be raised in the form of new stock issues (externally raised equity), retained earnings (internally generated equity), or increases in debt. Cooperatives, because of their unique user-based ownership and the resulting nonmarketability of their stock, are believed to suffer from restrictions on the availability of the two equity sources of capital. Cooperatives are thus viewed as "equity bound" and are thought to rely more heavily on debt financing than comparable IOFs (see Chapter 2).

In this research we have found that, contrary to expectations, the debt-to-assets ratios for cooperatives were not higher than for comparable IOFs (see Chapter 5). This unexpected behavior of debt levels in cooperatives may be attributable to two factors: (a) cooperatives face difficulties borrowing all they need, because commercial banks are uncomfortable with their "unorthodox" ownership structure; (b) cooperatives have lower investment needs than IOFs because they maintain lower rates of growth. Yet cooperatives in two industries – dairy and food processing – were found to grow at the same rate as comparable IOFs: around 10 percent per annum based on fixed assets (see Chapter 5). In another study, cooperatives in the food sector were actually found to have higher growth rates than comparable IOFs (Chen, Babb, and Schrader 1985).

Already this evidence questions the validity of the hypothesis of "equity starvation" in cooperatives. Yet this evidence was obtained by looking at total debt and equity levels of cooperatives in only two industries, without examining the year-by-year sources of growth financing. In this research, we use a substantially larger sample of U.S. agricultural cooperatives drawn from a wider range of industries and determine the proportions of equity and debt used by cooperatives to finance their growth. The cooperative sources of growth financing are then compared to the financing mix of investor-owned corporations as represented by the nonfinancial business sector of the U.S. economy. The present study thus examines more carefully than before the evidence to support or refute the hypothesis of "equity starvation" in cooperatives.

6.1. Methodology

For this study, growth is defined as the increase in the total assets in a particular year. By the basic balance-sheet equation,

$$dTA_{it} = dTL_{it} + dEQ_{it} \qquad (1)$$

where dTA_{it} is the change in total assets, dTL_{it} is the change in total liabilities (debt), and dEQ_{it} is the change in equity. The subscripts "it" denote cooperative i in year t. The left-hand side of Eq. (1) represents the uses of funds or the total investment; the right-hand side represents the sources of funds: increase in debt and increase in equity net of redemption. The growth measures calculated in Eq. (1) are based on current-year changes. These sources and uses components are therefore relatively unbiased by the historical accounting conventions that unavoidably affect the debt to equity ratios used in previous studies.

Eq. (1) can be broken down into more detailed components of sources and uses of funds, thus:

$$dFA_{it} + dCA_{it} = dCL_{it} + dLT_{it} + dEQ_{it} \qquad (2)$$

Among the uses of funds, dFA_{it} is the change in net fixed assets (capital expenditure net of depreciation) and dCA_{it} is the change in current assets (related to investment in working capital). Among the sources of funds, dCL_{it} is the change in current liabilities (short-term debt and suppliers' credit) and dLT_{it} is the change in long-term debt. The change in equity dEQ_{it} is made up of additions to retained earnings in all forms (both unallocated and allocated) plus new equity contributed by members, less any redemption of equity. Depreciation is not included among the sources, because the change in equity is based on reported retained earnings, which are calculated after depreciation expense. The sources and uses for cooperatives are thus calculated on the basis of book values, not cash flows.

The sources and uses components are expressed in proportion of total investment by dividing both sides in Eqs. (1) and (2) by dTA_{it}. The sources of funds in the right-hand side of Eqs. (1) or (2) divided by dTA_{it} indicate the proportions of growth financed by debt and equity. The sources and uses proportions for each year were averaged over all cooperatives with positive growth in that year. Annual observations with negative growth were omitted, because the sources proportions calculated with a negative change of total assets in the denominator are difficult to interpret. This analysis therefore focuses on growth and ignores contraction.

The sample for the analysis of cooperatives consists of the audited financial reports of 60 U.S. regional agricultural cooperatives with complete observations for the 15-year period 1973-1987. The sample includes dairy, food, grain, and farm supply cooperatives with 1987 average sales of around $400 million, which is similar to the sales volume of the top 100 U.S. cooperatives surveyed by the Agricultural Cooperative Service (Kane 1988).

6.2. Sources of Growth for Cooperatives

Table 6.1 presents the sources and uses proportions averaged over the cooperatives for each year during the period 1973-1987. It is apparent that the equity component in the financing of cooperative annual investments is by no means negligible: the annual increase in assets financed with equity ranges from a low of 21 percent to a high of over 69 percent. The mean equity financing proportion over the entire 15-year period is 45.4 percent of total investment, with a standard deviation of 14.7 percent. Cooperatives in this study thus finance nearly half of their growth with equity, even after taking care of all redemption outflows. Figure 6.1 illustrates the equity and debt proportions in the financing of cooperative growth.

New debt was raised by the cooperatives in this study mainly in the form of current liabilities. As indicated in Figure 6.1 and Table 6.1, most of the increase in debt financing is short-term, while the long-term debt component is relatively small. In three of the 15 years (1983, 1986, and 1987) there was a decrease in long-term debt. In these years, current liabilities increased not only to finance the new investment but also to adjust the debt structure to more short-term loans.

Cooperatives in this study apparently use permanent equity funds rather than debt to finance the increase in their long-lived capital assets. The close match between the equity financing component and the capital expenditure component of total investment is illustrated in Figure 6.2, where the time series indicating the proportions of equity and capital expenditure are seen to be intertwined. The difference between the equity financing proportions in the source accounts and the capital expenditure proportions in the uses accounts of cooperatives is not statistically significant at 0.10 level, both by the standard t-test and by the Wilcoxon nonparametric test.

6.3. Comparison of Cooperative and IOF Financing of Growth

The financing proportions of cooperatives are compared to the sources and uses data from the summary statements of savings and investment of U.S. nonfinancial corporations published in the Federal Reserve System's Flow of Funds Accounts (Board of Governors). These are aggregated data for nonfinancial corporate businesses in manufacturing, trade, and service industries. Farms (both corporate and noncorporate) are excluded from this category. The Federal Reserve System's sample is sufficiently large and general to be used as a proxy for the nonfinancial corporate sector of the U.S. economy. Insofar as most corporate businesses in this sample are IOFs, these flow of funds data provide a relevant reference or benchmark against which the behavior of cooperatives may be judged.

Table 6.2 presents the mean proportions of sources and uses of funds for the U.S. nonfinancial corporations, based on Federal Reserve System aggregated data. The Flow of Funds Accounts data are published on a cash flow basis. Adjustment to book values is made by subtracting the depreciation charges and the inventory valuation adjustment from the published figures for total internal funds on the sources side and from the changes in fixed assets and inventory on the uses side. The sources and uses proportions calculated after this adjustment (Table 6.2) are definitionally comparable to the proportions calculated from the annual reports of the cooperatives (Table 6.1).

TABLE 6.1: Sources and Uses of Funds: Means of 60 Agricultural Cooperatives, 1973-1987 (percent of total investment)

	1973	1974	1975	1976	1977	1978	1979	1980	1981	1982	1983	1984	1985	1986	1987
1. USES															
Capital expenditure	10.4	30.9	58.6	55.7	44.8	45.3	54.4	35.2	38.8	108.0	-4.1	32.2	24.4	23.1	25.7
Investment in current assets	89.6	69.1	41.4	44.3	55.2	54.7	45.6	64.8	61.2	-8.0	104.1	67.8	75.6	76.9	74.3
Total uses	100.0	100.0	100.0	100.0	100.0	100.0	100.0	100.0	100.0	100.0	100.0	100.0	100.0	100.0	100.0
2. SOURCES															
Increase in short-term debt	71.0	44.1	24.1	25.9	20.5	36.7	58.0	49.4	58.5	10.7	78.1	20.7	34.3	109.1	79.2
Increase in long-term debt	3.8	11.8	8.2	15.6	28.4	7.4	1.4	19.4	6.7	19.9	-14.5	41.1	10.9	-30.1	-32.3
Increase in debt	74.9	55.9	32.3	41.4	48.9	44.1	59.4	68.9	65.2	30.6	63.6	61.8	45.2	79.0	46.9
Increase in equity	25.1	44.1	67.7	58.6	51.1	55.9	40.6	31.1	34.8	69.4	36.4	38.2	54.8	21.0	53.1
Total sources	100.0	100.0	100.0	100.0	100.0	100.0	100.0	100.0	100.0	100.0	100.0	100.0	100.0	100.0	100.0

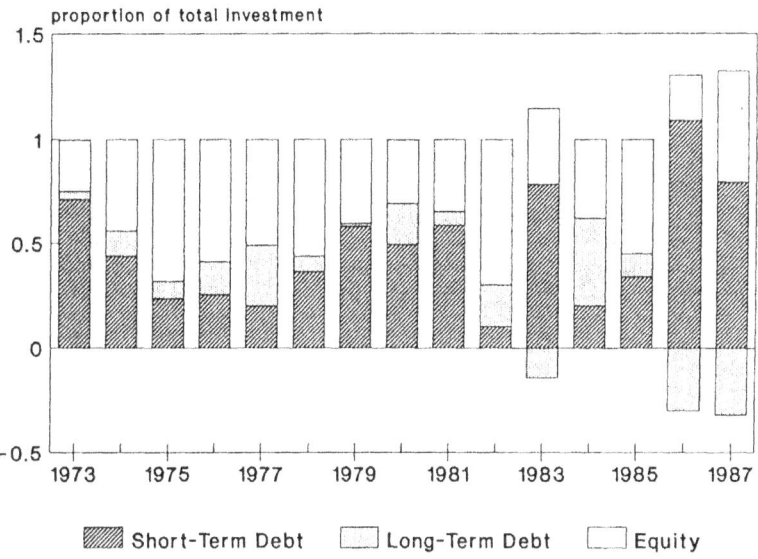

Figure 6.1. Mean sources of cooperatives, 1973-1987.

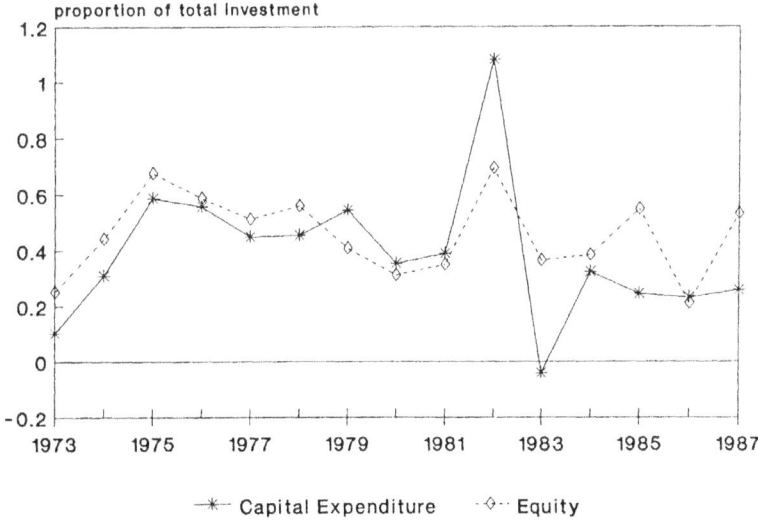

Figure 6.2. Capital expenditure and equity financing proportions of cooperatives, 1973-1987.

TABLE 6.2: Sources and Uses of Funds: Nonfinancial Corporations (percent of total)[a]

	1973	1974	1975	1976	1977	1978	1979	1980	1981	1982	1983	1984	1985	1986	1987
1. USES															
Net capital expenditure[b]	27.3	30.3	47.9	39.2	42.0	39.0	29.6	38.2	44.5	74.0	25.7	30.5	40.9	25.0	12.6
Investment in current assets[c]	72.7	69.7	52.1	60.8	58.0	61.0	70.4	61.8	55.5	26.0	74.3	69.5	59.1	75.0	87.4
Total uses	100.0	100.0	100.0	100.0	100.0	100.0	100.0	100.0	100.0	100.0	100.0	100.0	100.0	100.0	100.0
2. SOURCES															
Increase in short-term debt[d]	9.2	15.0	35.1	20.5	19.8	14.7	7.6	10.9	19.3	-9.6	12.0	32.3	60.1	87.4	67.3
Increase in long-term debt	55.2	49.6	-4.8	24.7	33.9	46.3	48.5	38.0	45.5	60.5	45.4	70.8	67.9	50.1	39.8
Increase in debt	64.4	64.5	30.3	45.1	53.7	61.0	56.1	48.9	64.9	50.9	57.4	103.1	128.0	137.4	107.1
Increase in equity[e]	35.6	35.5	69.7	54.9	46.3	39.1	43.9	51.1	35.1	49.1	42.6	-3.1	-28.0	-37.4	-7.1
Total sources	100.0	100.0	100.0	100.0	100.0	100.0	100.0	100.0	100.0	100.0	100.0	100.0	100.0	100.0	100.0

a Columns may not add up exactly due to rounding.
b Increase in net fixed assets, after depreciation charges.
c Includes increase in inventories at book value, without Inventory Valuation Adjustment
d Includes increase in accounts payable.
e Net equity issues plus retained earnings.
Source: "Sector Statements of Saving and Investment: Nonfinancial Corporate Business, Excluding Farms," *Flow of Funds Accounts*, Board of Governors of the Federal Reserve System, Division of Research and Statistics, various quarterly issues, pp. 10-11.

Equity Financing

Figure 6.3 plots the proportion of equity financing for both nonfinancial corporations and cooperatives. The two series are statistically indistinguishable during the period 1973-1983: the average equity financing proportion for this period are 46.8 percent of total investment for cooperatives and 45.7 percent for nonfinancial corporations, with standard deviations of 14.8 percent and 10.4 percent, respectively. From 1984, however, the equity financing component of nonfinancial corporations drops dramatically to negative values, while that of cooperatives continues at the same level as in prior years.

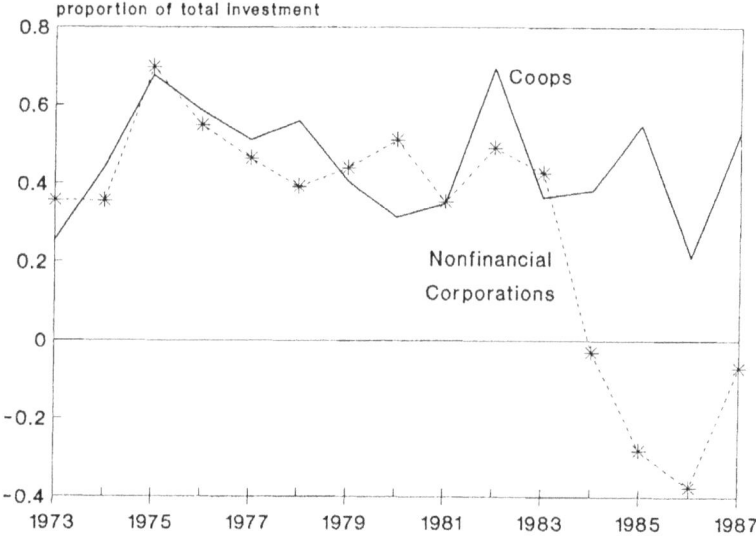

Figure 6.3. Equity financing proportions of cooperatives and IOFs.

Closer examination of the data in Flow of Funds Accounts indicates that the negative equity financing proportions of nonfinancial corporations are attributable to persistently negative amounts of new stock issues since 1984. Although the nonfinancial corporations in aggregate continued to report profits and the retained earnings remained positive, no new equity was issued on average: instead, the IOFs engaged in extensive stock repurchases, adjusting their capital structure toward higher leverage (Brealey and Myers 1991).

Debt Financing

The reduction of equity financing of nonfinancial corporations since 1984 has been accompanied by an increase in long-term debt financing without noticeable changes in the component of short-term loans. Nonfinancial corporations are evidently adjusting their capital structure shifting toward higher permanent debt levels, and the negative equity financing proportions are an indication of a long-term strategy.

TABLE 6.3: Sources and Uses Components: Averages for 1973-1983 and 1973-87 (percent of total investment; standard deviations in parentheses)

		1973-1987		1973-1983	
		Cooperatives	Nonfinancial corporations	Cooperatives	Nonfinancial corporations
1	USES				
	Capital expenditure	38.9 (25.6)	36.5 (13.9)	43.4 (28.7)	39.8 (13.5)
	Investment in current assets	61.1 (25.6)	63.5 (13.9)	56.6 (28.8)	60.2 (13.5)
2	SOURCES				
	Increase of equity	45.4. (14.7)	28.5* (31.8)	46.8 (14.8)	45.7 (10.4)
	Increase of short-term debt	48.0 (27.6)	44.8 (18.3)	43.4 (21.8)	40.3 (17.9)
	Increase of long-term debt	6.5* (19.8)	26.8* (25.9)	9.8 (11.4)	14.1 (10.9)
	Increase of total debt	54.6. (14.7)	71.5* (31.8)	53.2 (14.8)	54.3 (10.4)

* Differences between cooperatives and nonfinancial corporations significant at 0.1 level.

The differences between short-term debt proportions of cooperatives and nonfinancial corporations are not statistically significant over the entire period. The differences between long-term debt proportions of cooperatives and nonfinancial corporations, while statistically insignificant up to 1983, become statistically significant at 0.10 level when the years 1984-1987 are added to the time series. Nonfinancial corporations have been using significantly more long-term debt financing than cooperatives since 1984.

Table 6.3 presents a summary of the sources and uses proportions of cooperatives and nonfinancial corporations, averaged over the 15-year period 1973-1987. The averages for the 11-year subperiod 1973-1983 are also presented, because of the dramatic change in IOF financing patterns since 1984.

6.4. Conclusion

Theoretical considerations suggest that cooperatives are liable to suffer from a shortage of equity capital. Yet the agricultural cooperatives in this study were found to finance on average almost half of their total investment with equity – not exactly a sign of equity starvation. Perhaps this is due to the special mechanisms of per-unit retains and allocated patronage refunds that successful cooperatives implement to broaden their equity retention opportunities and thus sustain their growth in a competitive environment. Or, perhaps, as suggested by Caves and Petersen (1986), the high equity financing proportions observed in these cooperatives are the result of the specific tax treatment of cooperatives that enlarges the stream of internal financing per dollar of net margin. In any event, the empirical evidence presented here, does not support the theoretical hypothesis that cooperatives are "equity bound".

Cooperatives were found to raise new debt mainly in the form of short-term borrowing. It has been argued that cooperatives may have difficulties borrowing long-term, because commercial banks are uncomfortable with the "unorthodox" ownership structure and the dynamic nature of cooperative equity associated with various retention and redemption plans (Cobia and Brewer 1989). There are no such difficulties in obtaining short-term credit for cooperatives, because it is normally backed by familiar liquid assets, such as inventories and receivables. This argument is consistent with our finding of generally low levels of long-term debt among dairy cooperatives (Parliament, Lerman, and Fulton 1990).

During the period 1973-1983, the proportion of total investment financed with equity in cooperatives was found to be statistically indistinguishable from the benchmark used to represent IOFs. This is again contrary to theoretical expectations, which claim that cooperatives will resort to more debt financing than IOFs. Since 1984, the nonfinancial corporations have followed a strategy of stock repurchases, which has resulted in a dramatic reduction in the financing of growth with equity, while the cooperatives have continued to finance growth with the same equity proportions as in prior years. This trend for the nonfinancial corporations is probably a manifestation of the leveraged buyout phenomenon that enjoyed popularity in mid-1980s. Cooperatives, as suggested by an anonymous reviewer, are protected by their structure and the nonmarketability of their equities, from the huge accumulation of debt that accompanies leveraged buyouts. Perhaps in addition to acting as a competitive yardstick (Nourse 1922) cooperatives perform another public-policy function by counteracting the borrowing excesses associated with leveraged buyouts.

The observation of high equity financing proportions among the sample of cooperatives does not, however, resolve unambiguously the hypothesis of equity constraints in cooperatives. Because of equity redemption schemes, some cooperative equity may be regarded as loans from members and it is left to future research to examine more closely the composition of cooperative equity with regard to new capital infusion, allocated earnings, and the actual redemption outflows. Also a more detailed study is needed of the comparative growth rates of cooperatives and IOFs in a wider range of industries than previously attempted. This analysis of growth should link the financing patterns of cooperatives with financing needs and shed further light on the hypothesis of capital starvation in cooperatives.

7. Performance of Regional Enterprises in Israel

Regional enterprises in Israel are user-owned associations of independent service cooperatives. The development of regional enterprises has mainly followed two models. Some regional enterprises pursued a conservative business strategy, focusing on the traditional service functions of agricultural cooperatives, such as produce sorting and packing, storage, and marketing. Other regional enterprises pursued vertical integration strategies, expanding into value-added processing. Expansion into value-added processing usually involved large-scale capital investments, financed mainly with debt. The investments in most cases did not prove sufficiently profitable and, following the macroeconomic change in interest rates in 1985/86, the processors found themselves in a much more difficult situation than the conventional service enterprises.

In this chapter, we analyze and compare the performance of two regional enterprises that pursued different business strategies. One regional enterprise is an association of traditional service cooperatives, while the other enterprise has added a value-added processing plant to its range of service facilities. Both enterprises are located in the same part of Israel – the potato country, and the processing plant was constructed to produce and market potato-based consumer goods.

7.1. Size and Efficiency

The data for the two enterprises cover the period 1966-1986. The potato processing plant was established in 1973, but even in prior years this regional enterprise (we call it the Processor) was known for its innovative activities that extended far beyond the traditional scope of agricultural service functions. The Processor was larger than the Service Enterprise both in total assets and in sales during most of the period. The Processor's assets increased markedly after the establishment of the new processing plant in 1973 and the ratio of the Processor's total assets to the total assets of the Service Enterprise fluctuated around 4 during the decade 1973-1982 (Figure 7.1). The Processor's sales, however, were less than double the sales of the Service Enterprise during this period (Figure 7.1).

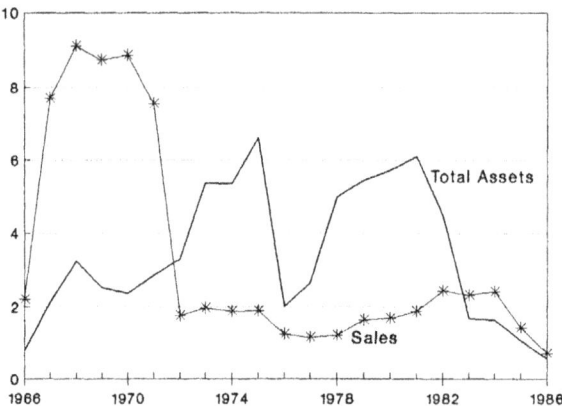

Figure 7.1. Size ratios of the Processor to the Service Enterprise, calculated on the basis of total assets and sales.

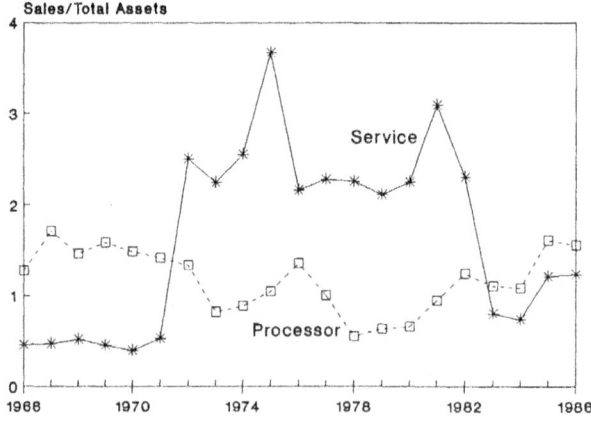

Figure 7.2. Sales to total assets ratios for the Processor and the Service Enterprise.

This was the first sign of trouble for the Processor: the new investments leading to a dramatic increase in total assets failed to produce a proportionate increase in sales. As a result, the Processor's efficiency ratio deteriorated: between 1973-1981 the ratio of sales to total assets was lower than between 1966-1972 and it returned to the pre-1973 level only after

1982 (Figure 7.2). More significantly, the Processor's efficiency ratio during most of the period (1972-1982) was much lower than the efficiency ratio of the Service Enterprise (Figure 7.2).

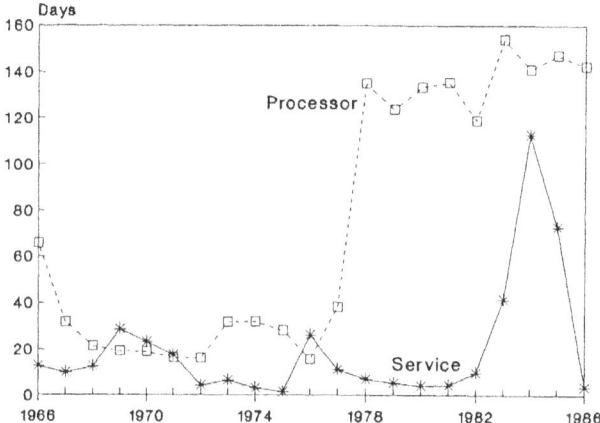

Figure 7.3. Inventory days for the Processor and the Service Enterprise.

Another measure of efficiency suggested in Table 2.1 is inventory turnover, calculated as the ratio of cost of sales to inventory. This turnover ratio can be recast as "inventory days", i.e., the number of days of sales in inventory, by taking the ratio of inventory to daily average cost of sales. Figure 7.3 plots the inventory days of the two regional enterprises. The Processor's inventory days were consistently higher than those of the Service Enterprise between 1972-1986. They increased dramatically after 1977, reaching 130-150 days between 1978-1986. Even if four-five months of inventory is normal for a manufacturer of consumer-food products, the difference compared to the normal pre-1973 level and the level maintained by the Service Enterprise provides an indication of the difficulties that the Processor is facing as a result of expansion into a new field.

7.2. Debt

The Processor has consistently operated with higher levels of debt than the Service Enterprise (Figure 7.4, panel (a)). The Processor also has consistently financed new investment with lower proportions of equity than the Service Enterprise (Figure 7.4, panel (b)). The ratio of outstanding debt to total sales (so-called "credit-years", see Chapter 8 below for a discussion of this debt measure) steadily rose between 1972-1986, exceeding by a large margin the credit-years of the Service Enterprise (Figure 7.4, panel (c)). This shows that the sales level lagged not only behind investment in assets, as we have seen above, but also behind the accumulating debt level of the

Processor. In other words, the Processor was overborrowing given its sales performance.

(a) LEVERAGE

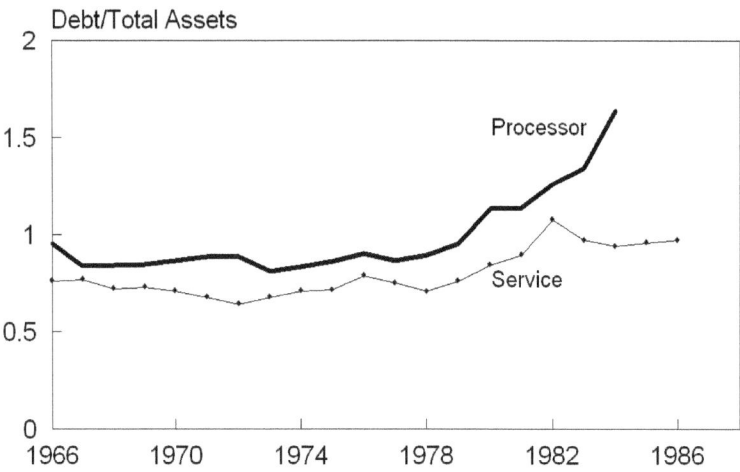

(b) EQUITY FINANCING PROPORTIONS

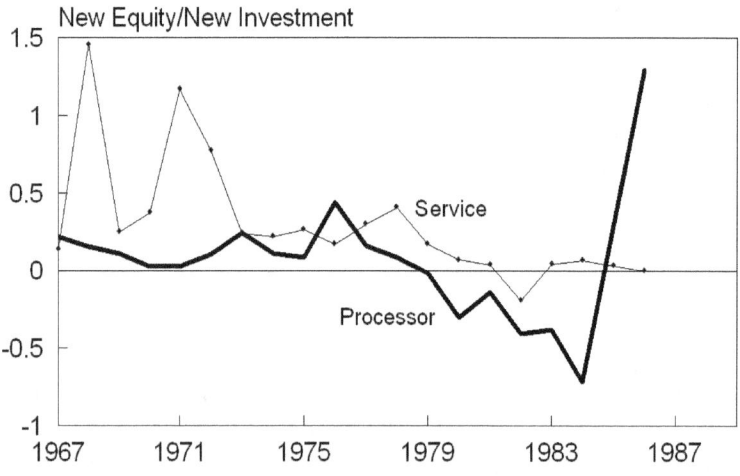

Figure 7.4. Debt measures for the Processor and the Service Enterprise: (a) Leverage, (b) Equity financing proportions.

(c) CREDIT-YEARS

(d) QUICK RATIO

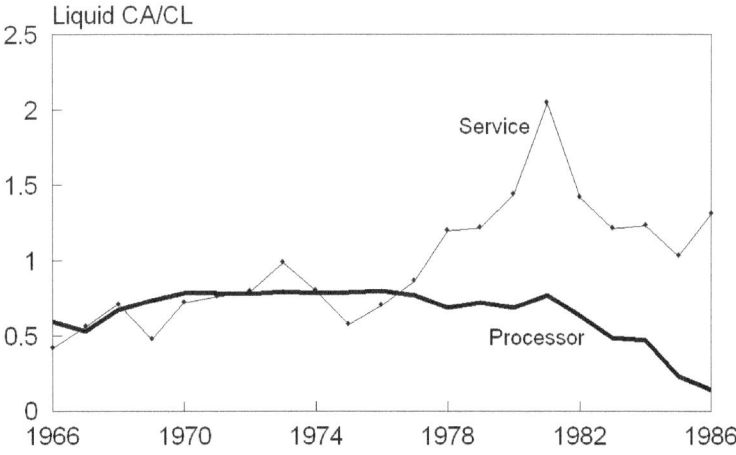

Figure 7.4 (continued). Debt measures for the Processor and the Service Enterprise: (c) Credit-Years, (d) Quick ratio.

Another indication of excessive reliance on borrowed funds is provided by the quick ratio in Figure 7.4, panel (d). The quick ratio is calculated as the ratio of liquid current assets (excluding inventory) to current liabilities (see Table 2.1). The Processor's quick ratio has been much lower than the quick ratio of the Service Enterprise since 1975. This is an indication of disproportionately high current liabilities, which are of course a form of debt.

Analysis of the composition of debt shows that current liabilities accounted for a higher proportion of total debt in the Processor than in the Service Enterprise. The difference was particularly pronounced between 1975-1980, when current liabilities represented nearly 75 percent of the Processor's total debt, compared to 50-60 percent in the Service Enterprise. A relatively large part of the Processor's debt was short term and had to be repaid or rolled over within one year, thus placing the cooperative under a considerable financial stress. This short-term debt, however, was mainly money owed to member-users (accounts payable to members) and suppliers' credit: both regional enterprises had very little short-term bank loans.

7.3. Profitability

Both regional enterprises reported operating profits in most of the years (i.e., profits before interest payments). Their situation, however, was totally different after financing expense. While the Service Enterprise had losing years, its absolute losses were small and it often reported substantial profits after interest (in 9 out of 20 years). The Service Enterprise retained these profits and thus managed to avoid dramatic erosion of its equity. The Processor, on the other hand, had zero profits after interest up to 1972 and began reporting increasing losses after interest in subsequent years (although it still showed operating profits in that period). The annual losses were retained against the equity account in the balance sheet and not distributed regularly to the members. As a result, the Processor's equity was rapidly wiped off and became negative. The Processor carried a negative equity on its books, and yet the management did not turn to the members with a request for infusion of new equity capital. The continuing losses forced the Processor to rely more and more on debt, which of course could not be repaid for lack of profits. The end result was the picture of general overborrowing that we have seen in Figure 7.4.

The favorable results reported for operating profits may be misleading in an inflationary environment, mainly because the costs are understated due to the use of historical depreciation. Current or replacement value depreciation is of course much higher than depreciation based on the original purchase cost of the assets. Adjustment of profits for current-value depreciation (Yacobi 1989) has had a much greater effect for the Processor than for the Service Enterprise, because of the Processor's greater "capital intensity". After current-value depreciation, the Processor shows continuous operating losses since 1973, the year when the potato processing plant was established, while the Service Enterprise had only 7 years of operating losses during the 20-year sample period. The conclusion is that the Processor really cannot justify the investments made in 1973 and that it should not continue operating at the present level of assets. This conclusion based on profitability considerations is of course consistent with the efficiency analysis conducted above.

7.4. Conclusion

The developments observed for the Processor may have several explanations. First, perhaps the investment was poorly chosen and the likelihood of the results justifying the means was small from the start. Second, perhaps the gestation period for an investment of this kind (a consumer-food plant) was long – probably longer than expected (the efficiency began showing signs of increase only ten years after the investment was made – see Figure 7.2). Third, perhaps a service cooperative did not have the managerial capability to deal with a consumer product that required a totally different and unfamiliar marketing approach.

The third possibility has conceptually the most difficult implications. It means that diversification into value-added processing may be dangerous for agricultural cooperatives. This conclusion is certainly supported by the Israeli experience far beyond the case study discussed in this chapter. There are some indications that it may be true also for U.S. cooperatives that expanded into food processing (see Chapter 4). Our preliminary findings only stress the need for further research into this interesting topic in order to decide between the views of "traditionalists", who maintain that agricultural cooperatives must restrict their activities to traditional service functions, and "progressivists", who maintain that the future lies in secondary value-added processing and vertical integration.

8. Comparison of Israeli Regional Enterprises and Investor-Owned Firms

Israeli agriculture experienced a severe financial crisis in 1986: debt levels that had been steadily increasing over the years finally exceeded the debt service capacity of the sector. Virtually the entire agricultural sector became technically insolvent. The crisis was precipitated by an abrupt exogenous increase in interest rates as a result of the government's anti-inflationary policy. Cooperatives, which account for over 80 percent of agricultural product in Israel, were hit much harder than the small private farming sector. It has therefore been suggested that the financial crisis may have been attributable to cooperative-specific factors.

The main facet of the financial crisis was heavy overborrowing by the agricultural cooperatives (see Chapter 1). This overborrowing may have been caused by the moral-hazard behavior inherent to cooperative organizations (see Chapter 2). Moral hazard increases the willingness to take risks, and this factor may have encouraged the cooperatives to borrow beyond the bounds of prudence. An additional cooperative-specific factor that may have contributed to overborrowing is the traditionally assumed shortage of equity capital in cooperatives (see Chapter 2). Because of their patron-based ownership structure, cooperatives are unable to raise equity from outside investors, while members exert pressure for immediate distribution of earnings through adjustment of costs and prices. The resulting equity shortage suggests that cooperatives may be forced to finance growth with relatively high proportions of debt, ultimately leading to excessive borrowing.

The hypothesis that overborrowing was produced by cooperative-specific factors can be tested by comparing the debt levels of cooperatives to those of non-cooperative, or investor-owned, firms (IOFs). Another possible test is to compare the debt levels of Israeli cooperatives to those of cooperatives in a culturally different environment, such as the U.S.

The Israeli agricultural cooperatives are structurally much more heterogeneous than cooperatives in other countries. A large segment of the Israeli cooperative agriculture is represented by production cooperatives (kibbutzim and moshavim), which are without obvious parallels in developed Western countries and are difficult to compare to business firms because of their unique social structure. The regional service cooperatives, on the other hand, are structurally and functionally similar to input purchasing and product marketing cooperatives in the U.S. and other Western countries and are moreover organized, at least on the surface, as business firms. In the interest of comparability with IOFs and with other countries, this research primarily focused on the performance of the Israeli regional enterprises in the kibbutz subsector.

The data used are described in Chapter 3 and the methodology is on the whole the same as in other parts of this research. Since the main objectives in this research is to compare the performance of cooperatives and IOFs, we accordingly evaluate cooperative performance using financial ratios based on audited financial statements. This methodology ensures comparability of data for cooperatives and IOFs, but admittedly it restricts the view of the cooperatives to a variant of a classical firm (see Chapter 2, Sec. 2.3 for alternative measures for performance evaluation of cooperatives).

8.1. Capital Structure

Theoretical considerations suggest that the capital structure of cooperatives will be biased toward a relatively high proportion of debt (see Chapter 2). The proportion of debt in the capital structure of a firm can be measured by the leverage ratio, calculated as the ratio of the total reported debt to total assets. It shows how much of the capital stock of a firm is financed with debt. The higher the leverage, the higher is the probability of failure and bankruptcy, and thus the higher the financial risk of the firm. Firms with a relatively low financial leverage are viewed as conservative and safe, while firms with a relatively high leverage are regarded as risky.

Figure 8.1 plots the leverage of Israeli cooperatives and IOFs between 1967-1987 (the leverage curve for coops plots the median debt-to-total assets ratio for the sample of regional enterprises). The Israeli cooperatives are seen to finance on the whole a higher proportion of their assets with debt than the IOFs. The average debt ratio for Israeli coops over the entire period is 0.83, while the average debt ratio for IOFs is 0.67. The debt ratio for cooperatives increased rapidly after 1977, in a period of high inflation and cheap credit, while the IOFs continued to finance with debt the same (or even lower) proportion of their assets as previously. This is consistent with the general growth of agricultural debt compared to industrial debt in that period (see Chapter 1, Figure 1.1).

The median debt levels of the regional enterprises contracted abruptly following the 1985/86 financial crisis, when the banking system imposed a severe credit crunch on the entire agricultural sector. This behavior of the debt levels in regional enterprises after 1985 is at variance with the behavior of the debt levels in the agricultural sector as a whole, which continued to increase at an accelerated rate after 1985 (see Chapter 1, Figure 1.1). The regional enterprises included in the sample apparently had sufficient reserves and sufficient profitability to repay their debt as it fell due, while the banks refused to let them roll it over. This may be the reason why the regional enterprises in the kibbutz subsector actually managed to survive the financial crisis and on the whole continue functioning to this day. It were mainly the other components of the Israeli cooperative agriculture that found themselves in default of their debt.

8.2. Alternative Measures of Debt

Leverage in this chapter is calculated as the ratio of total liabilities (the stock of outstanding debt) to the capital stock of the firm (i.e., debt and equity combined), and not to total equity alone, as in previous chapters. Stock ratios may be biased by historical accounting conventions in an inflationary environment. While debt is reported in current money terms, the fixed assets are reported at their historical purchase cost, and are therefore understated. Undervaluation of reported fixed assets causes undervaluation of reported equity and distorts equity-based ratios (on historical accounting biases and ways of correcting them, see Lerman 1989; Levy and Lerman 1987). Fixed assets, however, are only part of the total assets of the firm, and the remaining part (current assets) are reported in current money terms, like debt. The use of total assets in the denominator of the leverage ratio therefore reduces the historical accounting bias (without eliminating it altogether).

One of the ways to avoid historical accounting biases in an inflationary environment is to measure debt levels by so-called credit-years, calculated as the ratio of outstanding debt (total liabilities) to annual sales. Here, both the denominator and the numerator of the ratio are in current values and the sales figures are biased at most by half the annual inflation rate. This debt level measure provides an indication of the number of years it should take to pay off the outstanding debt: it is simply equal to the number of repayment years if we assume that all sales income is used to pay off debt and is proportional to the number of repayment years if a fixed percentage of sales is used for repayment.

Another technique to correct for possible historical accounting biases is to examine flow measures, and not stock measures. Flows are less susceptible to inflationary biases: the flows represent changes in assets and in debt that occurred during a single year, and the fixed asset component of the flows is distorted by less than a single year's inflation rate. Flow analysis estimates the percentage of each year's investment financed by debt, which we call debt financing proportion (compare Chapter 6).

The annual flows are calculated by differencing the balance sheet data between successive years. From the basic balance sheet equation, we obtain for the flows in year t

$$\Delta TA_t = \Delta DEBT_t + \Delta EQ_t$$

The change in total assets ΔTA_t represents the total new investment in the current year (year t). Dividing both sides of the flow equation by ΔTA_t we obtain

$$\Delta DEBT_t/\Delta TA_t + \Delta EQ_t/\Delta TA_t = 1$$

The two components in the left-hand side represent the proportions of total investment financed with debt and with equity, respectively. The higher the proportion of new investment financed with new debt ($\Delta DEBT_t/\Delta TA_t$), the faster will be the increase of the firm's stock of total liabilities and the higher will be its debt level.

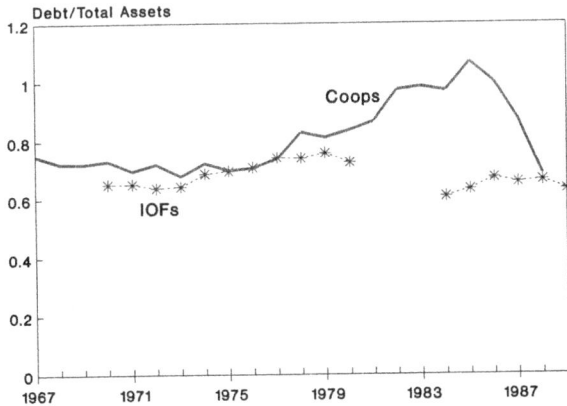

Figure 8.1. Leverage: Israeli Coops and IOFs

8.3. Credit-Years

Figure 8.2 compares the credit-years of Israeli regional cooperatives and IOFs (the curve for coops is again the median of the credit-years for our sample in each year). Since 1973, the credit-years of Israeli agricultural cooperatives have been consistently higher than the credit-years of the IOFs in the industry classification (including the food industry), although in earlier years the difference between Israeli cooperatives and IOFs was not as pronounced. The average credit-years for the period 1970-1987 were 0.87 for the Israeli cooperatives and 0.66 for the IOFs. In other words, 0.87 of the average annual sales of the cooperatives were needed to pay off the average outstanding depth, while the IOFs could pay off their outstanding debt by using only 0.66 of their annual sales. The difference between the two sets of data is statistically significant by the Wilcoxon test.

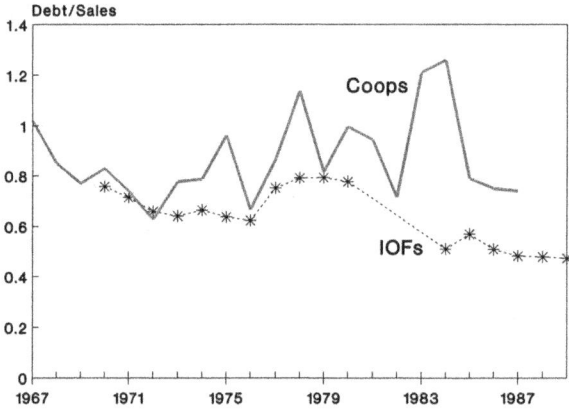

Figure 8.2. Credit-Years: Israeli Coops and IOFs

8.4. Debt Financing Proportions

Figure 8.3 plots the debt financing proportions of regional cooperatives and IOFs in Israel. Because of certain technical problems with IOF data, the results here are not as sharp as above, but it appears that after 1977 the cooperatives finance a higher proportion of their new investment with debt compared to IOFs. The average debt financing proportion for cooperatives is 0.82, while the corresponding proportion for IOFs is 0.71. This means that cooperatives on average financed with debt over 80 percent of new investment during the sample period, while IOFs financed around 70 of new investment with debt.

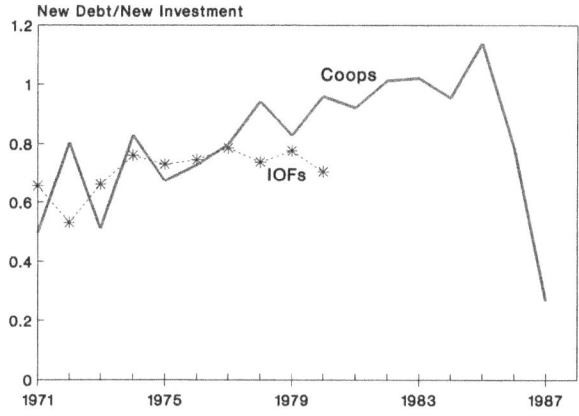

Figure 8.3. Debt Financing Proportions: Israeli Coops and IOFs

This finding is consistent with the observation that the debt levels of the cooperatives in the sample are on the whole higher than the debt levels of IOFs and that the gap began increasing after 1977 (see Figure 8.1). The dramatic reduction of new debt financing after 1985 is also consistent with the debt level findings in Figure 8.1.

8.5. Conclusion

Table 8.1 summarizes the three debt measures for Israeli regional cooperatives and IOFs. Regional cooperatives in Israel appear to rely more heavily on debt than IOFs by all measures. The credit-year and debt flow results indicate that the general qualitative picture of higher debt levels for the Israeli cooperatives compared to IOFs (Figure 8.1) is not the result of historical accounting biases that depress the reported value of the assets. The Israeli agricultural cooperatives financed a higher proportion of their annual investment with borrowed funds, and this inevitably led to accumulation of outstanding debt, as reflected in increasing leverage.

TABLE 8.1: Debt Measures for Regional Cooperatives and IOFs in Israel

Ratio	Cooperatives	IOFs
Leverage: Debt to Total Assets	0.83	0.67
Credit-Years: Debt to Annual Sales	0.87	0.64
Debt Financing Proportions: New Debt to New Investment	0.82	0.71

These findings are consistent with the theoretical expectations, which predict that moral hazard behavior and "equity starvation" due to horizon problems and nonmarketability of stock will cause cooperatives to rely more heavily on debt than IOFs (see Chapter 2, Table 2.1). The Israeli results are at variance with the results for U.S. regional cooperatives, whose debt levels and debt financing proportions are not higher than those of IOFs (see Chapter 5).

9. Comparison of Agricultural Cooperatives in the U.S. and Israel

The objectives of this research called for comparisons of the performance of agricultural cooperatives and investor-owned firms (IOFs) in two culturally different environments, as represented by the U.S. and Israel. The comparisons have revealed, for instance, that Israeli cooperatives tend to borrow more than the Israeli IOFs (see Chapter 8), while the evidence for U.S. cooperatives indicates that they definitely do not borrow more than comparable IOFs (see Chapter 5). The last stage of the research is to compare the performance of Israeli regional cooperatives to that of U.S. regionals. The present chapter compares the borrowing behavior of cooperatives in the U.S. and Israel.

9.1. Capital Structure

Capital structure, as in the previous chapter, is measured by the ratio of total liabilities to total assets (the reasons for the use of this leverage ratio in preference to the ratio of total liabilities to total equity is explained in Chapter 8). The higher the leverage, the higher is the probability of failure and bankruptcy, and thus the higher the financial risk of the firm.

Figure 9.1 shows the leverage of U.S. and Israeli agricultural cooperatives between 1967-1987. The leverage curves plot the median leverage estimated each year for the respective samples. The U.S. agricultural cooperatives have maintained a fairly constant median leverage of around 64 percent since 1970. This means that on average 64 percent of their assets are financed with debt from various sources (long-term debt, short-term loans, suppliers' credit), while the remaining 36 percent is financed with equity, or own capital. The median leverage of Israeli regional cooperatives was higher to start with – over 70 percent of total assets between 1967-1977; after that, the debt levels in Israel literally took off, rising steeply from 74 percent in 1977 to 107 percent in 1985, on the eve of the financial crisis. A debt ratio of over 100 percent means that Israeli agricultural cooperatives on average had a negative equity at that time, and they had to borrow to finance all their productive assets (100 percent) plus the accumulated deficit. The nonparametric Wilcoxon rank test shows that the difference between the median leverage series in U.S. and Israeli cooperative is statistically significant.

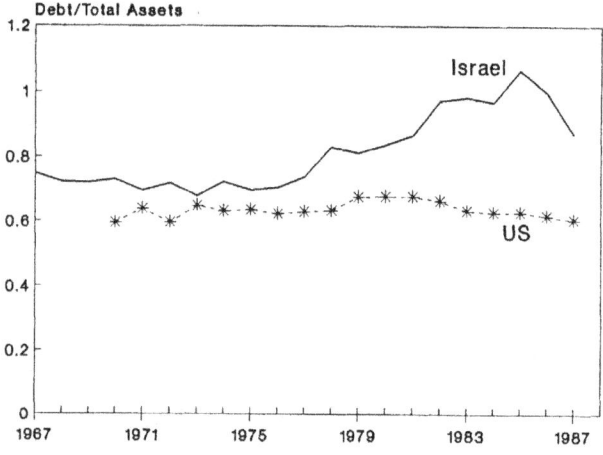

Figure 9.1. Leverage: Israeli and U.S. Cooperatives

9.2. Credit-Years

Credit-years are defined as the ratio of total debt to annual sales. The rationale for the use of credit-years as an alternative debt measure is outlined in Chapter 8. This debt measure provides an indication of the number of years it should take to pay off the outstanding debt.

Figure 9.2 shows the credit-years for U.S. and Israeli agricultural cooperatives between 1967-1987. The two curves plot the median credit-years estimated each year for the respective samples of cooperatives. The debt level of the Israeli cooperatives as measured by credit-years is consistently and significantly higher than the debt level of the U.S. cooperatives. The average credit-years for the period 1970-1987 was 0.87 for the Israeli cooperatives and 0.31 for the U.S. cooperatives. In other words, U.S. cooperatives could repay their total outstanding debt by using only 31 percent of their average annual sales, while the Israeli regional enterprises would need to allocate 87 percent of the average annual sales to pay off the average outstanding depth. The difference between the two sets of data is statistically significant by the Wilcoxon test.

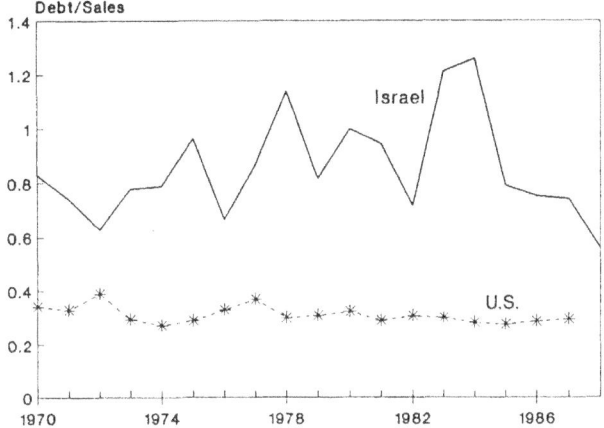

Figure 9.2. Credit-Years: Israeli and U.S. Cooperatives

9.3. Debt Financing Proportions

The two previous debt level measures – leverage ratio and credit-years – are based on the total outstanding debt of the cooperative. An alternative measure of indebtedness is based on flow data derived from year-to-year changes in the balance sheet. The flow analysis estimates the percentage of each year's investment financed by new debt. This debt financing proportion is defined as the ratio of the year-to-year change in total debt to the corresponding change in total investment ($\Delta DEBT_t/\Delta TA_t$), (see Chapter 8).

Figure 9.3. Debt Financing Proportions: Israeli and U.S. Cooperatives

Figure 9.3 shows that the Israeli cooperatives consistently financed a much higher proportion of their annual investment with debt than the comparable U.S. cooperatives. The difference between the two series is statistically significant by the nonparametric Wilcoxon test. In the period 1973-1985, the average annual debt financing proportion was 87 percent of total annual investment in Israel and only 53 percent in the U.S. After 1985, the debt financing proportion of the Israeli cooperatives declined dramatically: from 114 percent in 1985 to 27 percent in 1987 and to as low as 17 percent in 1988. This was the immediate result of the restrictions on the availability of new loans to agricultural cooperatives in the post-crisis period in Israel. The effect of the new credit restrictions is also seen in Figure 9.1: the total leverage of the Israeli cooperatives is observed to decline after 1985, when cooperatives found it impossible to roll over maturing debt in the crisis atmosphere. Despite the dramatic decline in debt financing of Israeli cooperatives after 1985, the average proportion over the 15-year period 1973-1987 was 82 percent, compared with only 55 percent in U.S. cooperatives.

The debt flow results indicate that the general qualitative picture of consistently higher debt levels for the Israeli cooperatives (Figure 9.1) is not the result of historical accounting biases that depress the reported value of the assets. The Israeli agricultural cooperatives consistently financed a much higher proportion of their annual investment with borrowed funds, and this inevitably led to accumulation of outstanding debt, as reflected in increasing leverage.

9.4. Conclusion

Table 9.1 summarizes the three debt measures for Israeli and U.S. cooperatives. There are obvious differences in the strategic behavior of cooperatives in different countries, as reflected in their capital structure and borrowing decisions. Israeli agricultural cooperatives appear to have consistently followed a much riskier financial strategy than comparable U.S. cooperatives. Israeli cooperatives also use more debt than IOFs (see Chapter 8), while U.S. cooperatives do not (see Chapter 5).

TABLE 9.1: Debt Measures for Regional Cooperatives in the U.S. and Israel

Ratio	Israel	U.S.
Leverage: Debt to Total Assets	0.83	0.64
Credit-Years: Debt to Annual Sales	0.87	0.31
Debt Financing Proportions: New Debt to New Investment	0.82	0.55

These difference can be attributable to cultural-environmental factors, such as differences in managerial attitudes, business norms, internal control structures, and government economic policies across countries, which are unquestionably reinforced by behavioral factors inherent to cooperative organizations. This suggests that even if the financial crisis in Israel was indeed precipitated by cooperative-specific factors, these factors are not universally active: their prominence or importance is largely a function of the cultural and business environment. While both Israeli and U.S. cooperatives may be structurally prone to moral hazard, this factor has had a much stronger impact on the cooperative business strategy in the Israeli cultural ethic than in the U.S.

Appendix. Estimating the Accounting Profitability of Pooling Cooperatives

A.1. Description of the Problem

The performance of a cooperative should properly be evaluated by measuring the benefits that the cooperative generates to its members. This is not practical, however, because member-level data are difficult to obtain. The research difficulties are further exacerbated by the fact that some cooperative-related benefits are of a public good or non-market nature (for a discussion of the non-market aspects of cooperatives and possible measures of performance, see Chapter 2, Sec. 2.3).

Because of these evaluation difficulties, researchers frequently measure the performance of cooperatives from cooperative-level accounting data. This approach restricts the evaluation of cooperatives to the IOF performance paradigm, and yet it relies on readily available standard data for which accepted interpretations are available. Recent examples of this approach are provided by the work of Schrader et al. (1985), as well as this research.

One of the standard performance measures for IOFs is profitability, defined as the rate of return to owners' equity and measured as the ratio of net profit to equity capital. The interpretation of this ratio for cooperatives is problematic: cooperatives have been viewed as zero-profit organizations (Helmberger and Hoos 1962), adjusting their payments or charges to members to achieve zero reported profit. Yet the results of this research show that the rate of return to equity of cooperatives is not less than that of IOFs in comparable industries (see Chapter 5). These empirical findings raise a question as to the role of profits in cooperatives and suggest that the profitability ratio should be included in the set of standard financial ratios for performance evaluation of cooperatives.

There is, however, a large group of agricultural marketing cooperatives for which the rate of return to equity cannot be calculated directly from published accounting data. These are the cooperatives that report "net proceeds" instead of a figure comparable to net profit or net margin. They operate as pooling cooperatives, commingling cost and sales figures across member producers and across products.

Marketing cooperatives that operate on a pooling basis fall into two categories based on the accounting treatment of cost of goods sold. Some pooling cooperatives follow the standard accounting convention of including the cost of members' raw products in their expenses and report the full cost of goods sold. The net profit or net margin in the income statement of these cooperatives is the residual return to members' equity, comparable to the net profit reported by IOFs and nonpooling cooperatives. Other pooling cooperatives exclude from their reported expenses the value of the raw products supplied by members to the cooperative. The excess of sales over expenses, reported as "net proceeds" by this second group of cooperatives, represents both the cost of members' raw products and the residual return to members' equity. The net proceeds are therefore not comparable to net profit or net margins.

Because of this incomparability of the bottom line in the income statements, profitability measures are currently calculated only for pooling cooperatives that report the full cost of goods sold. For example, Touche Ross (1989) calculate profitability ratios only for the subgroup of marketing cooperatives that include members' raw products in the cost of goods sold; the Agricultural Cooperative Service (ACS), in its surveys of the top 100 cooperatives, specifically excludes from profitability calculations cooperatives that use "pooled accounting methods with no net margins reported" (Davidson and Kane 1988); the National Cooperative Business Association (1987) does not publish earnings figures for "marketing cooperatives operating on a pool basis". The number of such cooperatives is not negligible. In the 1987-1988 Touche Ross survey, 10 out of 19 marketing cooperatives did not include raw products in their cost of goods sold (Touche Ross 1989). Of the largest 100 cooperatives in the US, 11 did not report net margins in the 1980 ACS survey (Davidson, Street, and Wissman 1982), and 7 in the 1986 survey (Davidson and Kane 1988).

Yet the data necessary for estimating the cost of goods sold and hence the net margin are available in the financial statements of the pooling cooperatives. The purpose of this paper is to show how the standard accounting information published in the audited statements can be used to estimate the profitability of pooling cooperatives that do not include raw products in their reported costs.

A.2. Adjustment of Net Proceeds to Equivalent Net Profit

The two basic measures of profitability are the rate of return to assets and the rate of return to equity. In both cases, the return component used in profitability calculation includes the reported accounting profit, variously referred **to as net profit, net earnings, net income, or net margin. Net profit is defined as the excess of revenues over related expenses during the accounting period. Revenues are the sales of products and services generated by the firm during the accounting period, and "expenses are outflows...of assets or *incurrences of liabilities*...from delivering or producing goods" (FASB 1980, italics supplied). When a member delivers raw products to a marketing cooperative, the cooperative incurs a liability, which represents the cost of member's produce. When these products are sold (possibly after value-added processing), an expense is recorded equal to the amount of the liability previously created. This expense is conceptually part of cost of goods sold. However, how this product expense is valued and reported in the financial statement varies among pooling cooperatives.

Some cooperatives value the liability by paying their members the estimated market value of the raw products. These are the cooperatives that include raw products in their cost of goods sold and report net margins. The bottom line of their income statement is comparable to the standard net profit, which accrues to members in the form of allocated or unallocated retained earnings or extra payments in excess of the market value of their products.

Other cooperatives do not record their liability to members as a component of cost of goods sold, and instead report net proceeds, which is not comparable to the standard net profit. The practice may have originated in the past when some cooperatives dealt with members' products that had no alternative markets. Yet it persists today in cooperatives dealing with standard marketable products, which choose not to value the members' products at market on delivery date. These cooperatives append a separate section to the income statement, which details the distribution of the net proceeds to members. The distribution is typically in the form of cash, accounts payable to members, or retained earnings. The payments to members, whether in cash or as credits to members' accounts payable, discharge the cooperative's liability for the members' products and accordingly can be regarded as the raw product component of the cost of goods sold.

STANDARD FORMAT:

Net Sales	1000	
Cost of Goods Sold	800	(1)
Gross Profit	200	
Operating Expenses	100	(2)
Operating Profit	100	
Interest Expense	50	
Net Profit	50	(3)

RECONCILIATION:

Net Sales		1000	
Cost of Goods Sold:			
Production Costs	100 +		
Payments to members	700 +	800	
Gross Profit		200	(1)
Operating Expenses		100	(2)
Operating Profit		100	
Interest Expense		50	
Net Profit		50	(3)

STANDARD PROFITABILITY MEASURES: Rate of Return on Assets (ROA) = (3)/Total Assets; Rate of Return to Equity (ROE) = (3)/Equity

COOPERATIVES NOT REPORTING COST OF GOODS SOLD:

VARIANT I:

Net Sales	1000	
Production Costs	100 +	
Operating Expenses	100	
Interest Expense	50	
Net Proceeds	750	
Payments to Members	700 +	
Retained Earnings	50	

VARIANT II:

Net Sales	1000	
Production Costs	100 +	
Operating Expenses	100	
Interest Expense	50	
Net Proceeds	750	

Distribution to Patrons:

Cash payments	700 +
Allocated retained earnings	25
Unallocated retained earnings	25
Total	750

VARIANT III:

Net Sales	1000	
Production Costs	100 +	
Operating Expenses	100	
Interest Expense	50	
Net Proceeds	750	

Distribution to Patrons:

Cash payments	500 +
Due to patrons (Accounts Payable)	200 +
Allocated retained earnings	25
Unallocated retained earnings	25
	750

VARIANT IV:

Net Sales	1000	
Production Costs	100 +	
Operating Expenses	100	
Interest Expense	50	
Net Proceeds	750	

Statement of Amounts Due to Members:

Balance, Beginning of the Year	378
ADD: Net Proceeds	750 +
Total available for distribution	1128
LESS: Cash Payments	825
Allocated Retained Earnings	25 −
Unallocated Retained Earnings	25 −
Balance, End of the Year	253

Figure A.1. Income statement format of pooling cooperatives: estimation of cost of goods sold and reconciliation to standard format.

It may be assumed that payments to members roughly equal market prices for members' products over time. If producers were not paid the equivalent of market prices, they would no longer use the cooperative. Alternatively, if the cooperative consistently paid more than the market value for the products, it would attract an increased business volume and eventually would be unable to pay more than the market prices to members.

Figure A.1 illustrates typical income-statement formats of pooling cooperatives. The "standard format" represents cooperatives that include members' raw products in the cost of goods sold. This "standard format" is identical to conventional income statements, and profitability measures can be calculated in the usual way, as shown in the figure. The other four formats represent variants of income statements found in pooling cooperatives that do not include raw products in the cost of goods sold. Items that should be included in cost of goods sold are identified by + (and –) sign in each variant.

In variant I, the reported payments to members should be added to production costs to obtain an estimate of the cost of goods sold. For this variant, retained earnings are equivalent to net profit, and a separate note or statement in the financial reports usually details the distribution of the retained earnings.

In variants II and III, the payments to members and the allocated and unallocated retained earnings are shown explicitly in a statement of distribution. The only difference between these variants is that all the payments in variant II are in cash, while the payments in variant III are part cash and part credit to members' accounts payable, to be paid in cash at a later date.

While the first three variants present the distribution of net proceeds to members in the current year, variant IV presents a consolidated picture of the amounts due to members, including prior years and the balances carried forward to the next year. In this variant, part of cash payments represent discharge of liabilities incurred in previous years, while part of the current year's liabilities may be credited to the balance of accounts payable and not distributed as cash. Members' product costs may be calculated by subtracting the retained earnings (allocated and unallocated) from the net proceeds for the current year, as shown in Figure A.1.

The reconciliation panel in Figure A.1 summarizes the transformation of the four variants to the standard format. The cost of goods sold in the reconciled format includes the production costs, as originally reported, plus the adjustment items representing the cost of members' raw products, as identified in the four variants. In addition to the general formats of Figure A.1, the adjustment should include such technical items as quality incentive payments or payments to members due to meeting their patronage quota, which are obviously directly related to members' product cost. It should not include dividend payments and other amounts that are related to the equity account of the cooperative. The reconciled format in Figure A.1 is identical to the standard format, so that profitability measures can be calculated in a comparable way.

A.3. Application and Empirical Test of the Proposed Estimation Technique

The proposed technique for estimating the profitability of pool cooperatives that do not include raw products in their cost of goods sold was tested on a sample of 12 marketing cooperatives in the fruit and vegetable processing industry that operate on a pooling basis. The sample comprised six cooperatives that included members' raw products in their cost of goods sold (group A), and six cooperatives that included only production and processing costs in their cost of sales, treating raw product costs as part of payments to members (group B). The sample data consisted of audited financial statements for the 17-year period 1971-1987. All sample cooperatives had a similar mix of operations, with the only obvious difference between them provided by the accounting treatment of costs of sales. It was therefore expected that the profitability measures of the cooperatives in the two groups would be statistically similar when estimated on a comparable basis.

The technique described above was applied to convert the reported net proceeds to equivalent net margins for the six cooperatives in group B. The rate of return to equity (ROE) was then calculated for each of the 12 cooperatives for the years 1971-1987, using the ratio of net profit before tax to total reported equity. The median ROE and the interquartile range were determined for each year for group A and group B cooperatives separately. The ROE time series are presented in Figure A.2 (for detailed data see Table A.1): the shaded band is the interquartile range of the ROE of the group A cooperatives that follow standard accounting reporting, and the solid line with square markers is the median rate of return for the group B cooperatives that do not include raw products in their cost of goods sold.

The median ROE of group B cooperatives in Figure A.2 falls within the interquartile range of the group A cooperatives for most years. Thus, the adjustment procedure estimates rates of return to equity for cooperatives not reporting raw product costs that are comparable to rates of return to equity for "net-margin-reporting" cooperatives. The nonparametric Wilcoxon test (see, e.g., Daniel 1990) of the time series of the median ROE for the two groups of pooling cooperatives did not reject the hypothesis of equal median rates of return. The probability of the test statistic exceeding the observed value under the null hypothesis of equal median rates of return for the two groups was 0.76.

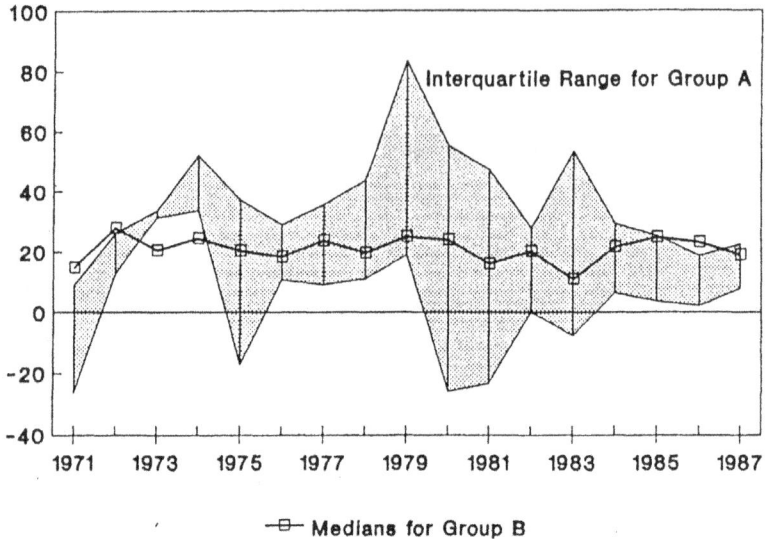

-□- Medians for Group B

Figure A.2. Median of adjusted rates of return on equity for cooperatives not reporting net margins (Group B) compared to interquartile range of rates of return on equity for cooperatives that report net margins (Group A), 1971-1987

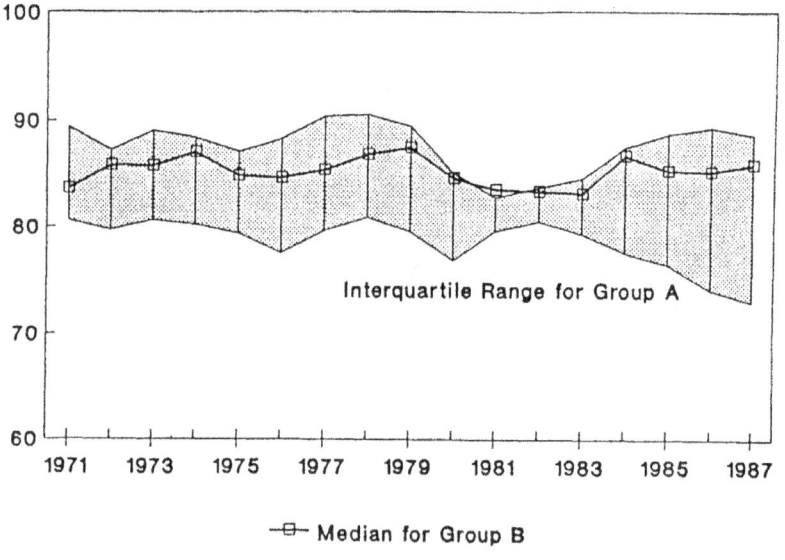

-□- Median for Group B

Figure A.3. Median of margin on sales for cooperatives not reporting net margins (Group B) compared to interquartile range of margin on sales for cooperatives that report net margins (Group A), 1971-1987

Part of the payments to members incorporated into cost of goods sold by the proposed adjustment technique may represent product costs from prior years pools. The empirical results indicate, however, that this departure from the matching principle of accounting does not have a significant effect on the profitability measure estimated for pool cooperatives that exclude raw products from their costs.

TABLE A.1: Rate of Return to Equity for Group A and Group B Cooperatives: Medians and Interquartile Range, 1971-1987

Year	Lower Quartile Group A	Median Group A	Median Group B	Top Quartile Group A
1971	-26.20	-8.60	14.88	9.01
1972	12.97	23.30	27.96	26.08
1973	31.30	32.25	20.48	33.58
1974	33.63	35.68	24.44	52.00
1975	-17.30	11.22	20.27	37.04
1976	10.74	21.21	18.39	28.96
1977	9.28	29.86	23.62	35.67
1978	11.23	25.16	19.69	43.70
1979	18.91	26.67	24.91	83.20
1980	-25.80	8.47	23.80	55.36
1981	-23.21	33.70	16.17	47.36
1982	0.00	25.37	20.09	27.78
1983	-7.70	11.43	11.02	53.52
1984	6.57	14.60	21.55	29.32
1985	3.75	11.60	24.78	25.28
1986	2.09	4.47	23.13	18.72
1987	7.92	14.39	18.89	22.43

The empirical justification of the technique relies on the assumption that, because of similarity in operations, group A and group B cooperatives are expected to have basically similar profitability levels. Unfortunately, it was impossible to cross-check the results by running a similar analysis on the "net proceeds" of the cooperatives in groups A and B: the data for net-margin-reporting cooperatives in group A do not separate the cost of goods sold into processing and product costs and it is therefore impossible to reconstruct net proceeds comparable to those reported by group B cooperatives. The similarity of the cooperatives in the two groups was therefore checked by analyzing a proxy profitability measure calculated as a margin on sales after operating, financing, and other expenses, excluding all components of cost of goods sold. These cost components are reported on a comparable basis by the cooperatives in both groups and the proxy measure was therefore based on raw data that did not require any adjustment.

The results of this analysis are presented in Figure A.3. Here again the median proxy measure for group B cooperatives falls within the interquartile range of this measure for group A cooperatives and the Wilcoxon test does not reject the hypothesis of equal medians for the two groups. This additional analysis supports the conjecture that the cooperatives in both groups can be expected to have equal profitability levels as measured by rate of return to equity and lends credence to the proposed adjustment technique.

A.4. Conclusion

Because of the similarity in their operations, cooperatives in both groups – those reporting net proceeds and those reporting net margins – can be expected to post similar measure of profitability in a competitive market. The results of this paper indicate that the profitability estimates obtained by the proposed adjustment procedure for cooperatives that do not report raw product costs are comparable to the profitability ratios of cooperatives that report conventional net margins. The empirical findings thus suggest that the procedure proposed in this paper may be used to estimate the profitability of a category of pool cooperatives that have previously been ignored.

Application of the proposed profitability estimation technique will enrich the data base for future research on cooperative financial performance through the inclusion of a substantial number of cooperatives for which no profitability measures were calculated in the past. It will also enable pooling cooperatives that do not report net margins to compare their profitability performance to other cooperatives and investor-owned firms.

References

Babb E.M. 1982. *Analysis of Grade B Milk Prices Paid by Wisconsin and Minnesota Dairy Plants*, Agricultural Experiment Station Bulletin 392, Purdue University.

Babb E.M., and M.F. Lang. 1985. "Implication of Comparative Performance of Cooperatives and Investor-owned Firms," in: L.F. Schrader and W.D. Dobson, eds., *Farmer Cooperatives for the Future: NCR-140 Research on Cooperatives and Extension Committee on Organization and Policy Published Proceedings*, Department of Agricultural Economics, Purdue University and USDA Agricultural Cooperative Service, pp. 12-16.

Biser L. and L. O'Day. 1984. *Growth and Trends in Cooperative Operations, 1951-81*, USDA Agricultural Cooperative Service, ACS Research Report Number 37, Washington, DC.

Board of Governors, Federal Reserve System, *Flow of Funds Accounts*, Washington, DC, various issues, pp. 10-11.

Boynton R.D. and E.M. Babb. 1982. *Farmers' Perceptions of the Comparative Performance of Cooperative and Proprietary Agribusinesses*, Station Bulletin 383, Department of Agricultural Economics, Purdue University, West Lafayette, IN.

Brealey R.A. and S.C. Myers. 1991. *Principles of Corporate Finance*, 4th ed., McGraw-Hill Book Co., New York.

Brookshire D.S., M.A. Thayer, W.D. Schulze, and R.C. D'Arge. 1982. "Valuing Public Goods: A Comparison of Survey and Hedonic Approaches." *American Economic Review* 72: 165-177.

Buch V. 1984. *Capital Stock Series in Israel 1960-1984*, Bank of Israel, Research Department, Jerusalem.

Buzzell R.D. and F.D. Wiersema. 1981. "Successful Share-Building Strategies," *Harvard Business Review* (Jan.-Feb.), p. 137.

Caves R.E. and B.C. Petersen. 1986. "Cooperatives' Tax Advantages," *American Journal of Agricultural Economics* 68: 207-213.

Chen K.-S., E.M. Babb, and L.F. Schrader. 1985. "Growth of Large Cooperative and Proprietary Firms in the US Food Sector," *Agribusiness* 1(2): 201-210.

Cobia D. W. and T. A. Brewer. 1989. "Equity and Debt," in: D. Cobia, ed., *Cooperatives in Agriculture*, Englewood Cliffs, NJ, Prentice-Hall, pp. 243-266.

Cobia D.W., J.S. Royer, R.A. Wissman, D.P. Smith, D.R. Davidson, S.D. Lurya, J.W. Mather, P.F. Brown, and K.P. Krueger. 1982. *Equity Redemption: Issues and Alternatives for Farmer Cooperatives*, U.S. Department of Agriculture, Agricultural Cooperative Service, ACS Research Report No. 23, Washington, DC.

Condon A.M. 1987. "The Methodology and Requirements of a Theory of Modern Cooperative Enterprise," in: J.S. Royer, ed., *Cooperative Theory: New Approaches*, U.S. Department of Agriculture, Agricultural Cooperative Service, ACS Service Report No. 18, Washington, DC, pp. 1-32.

Condon A. M. and P. Vitaliano. 1983. *Agency Problems, Residual Claims, and Cooperative Enterprise*, Cooperative Theory Working Paper No. 4, Department of Agricultural Economics, Virginia Polytechnical Institute and State University.

Copeland T.E. and J.F. Weston. 1983. *Financial Theory and Corporate Policy*, Addison-Wesley, Reading, MA.

Cotterill R. W. 1987. "Agricultural Cooperatives: A Unified Theory of Pricing, Finance, and Investment," in: J.S. Royer, ed., *Cooperative Theory: New Approaches*, U.S. Department of Agriculture, Agricultural Cooperative Service, ACS Service Report No. 18, Washington, DC, pp. 171-258.

Cummings R., D. Brookshire, and W. Schulze. 1986. *Valuing Environmental Goods: An Assessment of the Contingent Valuation Method*, Towtowa, Rowman and Allanheld.

Daniel W.W. 1990. *Applied Nonparametric Statistics*, PWS-KENT Publishing Company, Boston.

Davidson D.R. and M.D. Kane. 1988. *Top 100 Cooperatives, 1986 Financial Profile*, ACS Research Report No. 71, USDA Agricultural Cooperative Service, Washington, DC.

Davidson D.R., D.W. Street, and R.A. Wissman. 1982. *Top 100 Cooperatives, 1980 Financial Profile*, ACS Research Report No. 24, USDA Agricultural Cooperative Service, Washington, DC.

Enke S. 1945. "Consumer Cooperatives and Economic Efficiency," *American Economic Review* 35(1): 148-55 (March).

FASB. 1980. *Elements of Financial Statements of Business Enterprises*, FASB Statement of Financial Accounting Concepts No. 3, Financial Accounting Standards Board, Stamford, Conn.

Goodman A.C. 1989. "Identifying Willingness-to-Pay for Heterogeneous Goods with Factorial Survey Methods," *Journal of Environmental Economics and Management* 16: 58-79.

Helmberger P.G. and S. Hoos. 1962. "Cooperative Enterprise and Organization Theory," *Journal of Farm Economics* 44: 275-90 (May).

Jermolowicz A. and T. Kennedy. 1989. *Directory of Farmer Cooperatives*, U.S. Department of Agriculture, Agricultural Cooperative Service, ACS Service Report 22, Washington, DC.

Kane M. 1988. "Improved Ag Economy, Management Help Top 100 Co-ops Improve Returns to Members," *Top 100 Cooperatives: 1988 Financial Profile*, U.S. Department of Agriculture, Agricultural Cooperative Service, Washington, DC.

Kislev Y and A. Marvid. 1988. A Supply Cooperative of Moshavim: Plants, Economic Functioning and Finance [in Hebrew], Magnes Prees, Jerusalem. Israel

Koller F. (1972-73). "What are Issues Involved in Cooperative Growth?", *American Cooperation*, p. 147.

Lang M.F., E.M. Babb, R.D. Boynton, and L.F. Schrader. 1985. *Performance Dimensions for Cooperatives and Proprietary Firms: Perceptions and Research Priorities*, Indiana Agricultural Experimental Station Bulletin 281, Purdue University, West Lafayette, IN.

Lerman Z. 1989. "Capital Structure of Agricultural Cooperatives in Israel," *Yearbook of Co-operative Enterprise 1989*, Plunkett Foundation for Co-operative Research, Oxford, pp. 73-90.

LeVay C. 1983. "Agricultural Cooperative Theory: A Review," *Journal of Agricultural Economics* 34: 1-44.

Levy H. and Z. Lerman. 1985. "Testing P/E Filters by Stochastic Dominance Rules," *Journal of Portfolio Management* 11(2): 31-40 (Winter).

Levy H. and Z. Lerman. 1987. "Estimating the Cost of Capital Under Inflation − Israeli Industry, 1971-80," *Bank of Israel Economic Review* No. 59: 64-87 (May).

Mitchell R. and R. Carson. 1989. *Using Surveys to Value Public Goods: The Contingent Valuation Method*. Johns Hopkins Press, Baltimore, MD.

National Cooperative Business Association. 1987. *Special Report: 1986 Top 50 Agricultural Cooperatives*, Washington, DC.

Nelson J. 1979. "Airport Noise, Location Rent, and the Market for Residential Amenities," *Journal of Environmental Economics and Management* 6: 320-331.

Nourse E.G. 1922. "The Economic Philosophy of Cooperation," *American Economic Review* 12(4): 577-597 (December.

Parliament C., Z. Lerman, and J. Fulton. 1990. "Performance of Cooperatives and Investor-Owned Firms in the Dairy Industry," *Journal of Agricultural Cooperation* 5: 1-16.

Parliament C. and J. Taitt. 1989. *Mergers, Consolidations, Acquisitions: Effect on Performance of Agricultural Cooperatives*, Staff Paper P89-37, Department of Agricultural and Applied Economics, University of Minnesota, St. Paul, MN.

Ravenscraft D. and F.M. Scherer. 1987. *Mergers, Sell-offs, and Economic Efficiency*, Brookings Institution, Washington, D.C.

Robert Morris Associates. 1971-1988. *Annual Statement Studies*, Philadelphia, PA.

Rosenthal G. and H. Eiges. 2014. "Agricultural cooperatives in Israel," *Journal of Rural Cooperation* 42(1): 1-29.

Royer J.S. 1985. "Strategies for Capitalizing Farmer Cooperatives," in: L.F. Schrader and W.D. Dobson, eds., *Farmer Cooperatives for the Future: NCR-140 Research on Cooperatives and Extension Committee on Organization and Policy Published Proceedings*, Department of Agricultural Economics, Purdue University and USDA Agricultural Cooperative Service, pp. 83-90.

Schrader L.F. 1989a. "Economic Justification," in: D.W. Cobia, ed., *Cooperatives in Agriculture*, Prentice Hall, Englewood Cliffs, NJ.

Schrader L.F. 1989b. "Equity Capital and Restructuring of Cooperatives as Investor-Oriented Firms," *Journal of Agricultural Cooperation 4:* 41-53.

Schrader L.F., E.M. Babb, R.D. Boynton, and M.G. Lang. 1985. *Cooperative and Proprietary Agribusinesses: Comparison of Performance*, Purdue Agricultural Experiment Station Research Bulletin 982, Purdue University, West Lafayette, IN.

Sexton R. 1989. "Some Tests of the Economic Theory of Cooperatives: Methodology and Application to Cotton Ginning," *Western Journal of Agricultural Economics* 14: 56.

Smith V.K. and W. Desvouges. 1986. *Measuring Water Quality Benefits*, Kluwer-Nijhoff, Boston, MA.

Staatz J.M. 1987. "Farmers' Incentives to Take Collective Action via Cooperatives: A Transaction-Cost Approach." in: J.S. Royer, ed., *Cooperative Theory: New Approaches*, USDA Agricultural Cooperative Service, ACS Service Report Number 18, Washington, D.C.

Staatz J.M. 1989. *Farmer Cooperative Theory: Recent Developments*, USDA Agricultural Cooperative Service, ACS Research Report Number 84, Washington, D.C.

Touche Ross. 1989. *Financial Ratios for Food Processing Corporations and Agricultural Cooperatives, Fiscal Year 1987-1988*, San Francisco.

U.S. Department of Agriculture. 1987. *Cooperative Historical Statistics*, Agricultural Cooperative Service, Cooperative Information Report No. 1, Section 26, Washington, DC.

Van Dijk G. and C.P. Veerman. 1990. *The Philosophy and Practice of Dutch Co-operative Marketing*, Center for Agricultural Economic Research, Working Paper No. 9008, Rehovot, Israel.

Yacobi U. 1989. *A Comparative Study of Two Regional Cooperative Enterprises in the Negev*, MSc Thesis, Department of Agricultural Economics and Management, Hebrew University, Rehovot, Israel [in Hebrew, with English summary].

Zusman P. 1988. *Individual Behavior and Social Choice in a Cooperative Settlement*, Magnes Press, Jerusalem, Israel.

About the Authors

Zvi Lerman is Professor Emeritus of Agricultural Economics at the Hebrew University of Jerusalem. Since 1991 his research has focused on land reform and farm restructuring in transition economies, including agricultural cooperatives in former socialist countries. His research findings have been widely published in journals, books, and conferences. He has recently co-authored (with David Sedik and Csaba Csaki) a collection of articles on agricultural cooperatives in transition countries (LAP – Lambert Academic Publishing, 2016, ISBN 978-3-330-01568-5).

Claudia Parliament is Professor Emerita in the Department of Applied Economics, University of Minnesota. Her research interests include Cooperatives, Economic Development and Growth, and Economic Education. Awards: Schramm Leadership Award, National Association of Economic Educators (2013) Distinguished Diversity and Inclusion Award, CFANS (2013) and MN Extension (2012), Certificate of Recognition for Leadership to Minnesota K-12 Teachers in Economics, State of Minnesota, (2012), Global Engagement Award, University of Minnesota (2010).